THE INTIMACY FACTOR

Books in the Minirth-Meier Clinic Series

THE INTIMACY FACTOR

Dr. David Stoop & Jan Stoop

A JANET THOMA BOOK

THOMAS NELSON PUBLISHERS

NASHVILLE

Published in association with the literary agency of Alive
Communications, P.O. Box 49068, Colorado Springs, CO 80949.

Published in Nashville, Tennessee, by Thomas Nelson, Inc., and
distributed in Canada by Lawson Falle, Ltd., Cambridge, Ontario.

Scripture quotations are from THE NEW KING JAMES VERSION of the
Bible. Copyright © 1979, 1980, 1982, Thomas Nelson, Inc., Publishers.

Library of Congress Catalog Card Number 92-56468

ISBN 0-8407-7568-7

Printed in the United States of America

1   2   3   4   5   6   7   -   97   96   95   94   93   92

To all the couples we have met through counseling and at our retreats who have allowed us to share in their search for intimacy. They have enriched our lives and our own marriage and have taught us as well what it means to be a couple.

CONTENTS

PART FOUR:
The Building Blocks of a Loving Relationship

Appendix

Notes   253

PART ONE

Our Ability to Love and Be Loved

1

The Intimacy Puzzle

I DON'T KNOW what made me do it. The day was so beautiful and sunny, and the mountain roads were so inviting—and I guess I have always been fascinated with convertibles. Who would have thought a sunburn would be such an issue on our wedding day? I sure didn't. I guess I just didn't think ahead.

That day, July 20, 1957, everything was as Jan had dreamed it would be. The day was sunny and beautiful. The tiny white church with the steeple was decorated with fresh flowers. The bridesmaids' gowns were all adjusted, and Jan's hair was perfect. Jan remembers the sense of relief as the time of the wedding drew closer—all the details had come together without any last-minute crises.

We were married at a time when the tradition was important that the bride and groom did not see each other until the moment the bride entered on the arm of her father. As Jan walked down the aisle, she looked at her bridegroom and had the fleeting thoughts, *Why is his face so red? Is he sick? Does he do that when he gets nervous?*

Later, after we got in the car to head for the reception, my face was still red. She asked me why.

"Sunburn, I guess," I remember saying. There was little time to say much else, as the reception and the opening of the gifts seemed to take forever.

Later, when we looked at the pictures of the wedding, I could see why Jan had been so surprised at my appearance. While everyone else looked relaxed and moderately tanned, I stood out with a flaming red face. "Why?" Jan asked again. "Why? What were you thinking? Didn't you think about what would happen? How could you be so thoughtless and ruin our wedding pictures?"

I tried to explain my love of convertibles, and how I couldn't refuse my best man's offer to use his new Oldsmobile convertible to scout around for the place we would stay our wedding night. For two hours, I had enjoyed driving with the top down. How did I know I would get a sunburn? And wedding pictures? I never had a moment's thought about the wedding pictures.

As I talked, I began wondering, *How could Jan be so picky? How could she ruin our wedding day by thinking only about the pictures and not focusing on our being together? Did she let a little thing like sunburn interfere with her enjoyment of that very special day?*

Obviously, our concerns about the wedding were at opposite ends of the spectrum. And we have been surprised as we've continued down the path of our married life to discover how different our perspectives on most things are. We had no clue that what Jan thought was important would be completely different from what I felt important. Nor did we know that little misunderstandings could easily develop into deep and hurtful resentments.

Let's face it. Most of us try to figure out the problems after the fact. We don't think in advance about what might be if. . . . As with my sunburn, we end up trying to figure out our relationship issues after the fact—after we are married.

After the wedding we began the long, hard process of figuring out how we were going to deal with our anger and with the disappointments we had with each other. Patterns were set in motion during that first marital misunderstanding that lasted many years. Some were more difficult to change than others. Some were more painful than others. Disappointments are tough in any circumstance, but the disappointments faced when someone you have committed your life to "lets you down" can be devastating.

That day, more than thirty-five years ago, we started down the road that was supposed to lead to an intimate relationship. Sometimes our struggles nearly destroyed us. We look back at certain periods of time and marvel that we hung in there with each other. But there were also the other times, when the principles we were learning felt more understandable and the struggle wasn't as intense. We will share with you in this book some of the things we have learned that have helped us in our search for intimacy. But first, let's begin by defining the word *intimacy,* so we will have a common definition of our goal as partners in marriage.

Intimacy Defined

A simple definition of *intimacy* is "the joyful union that comes when two people learn together how to give love and how to accept love." Intimacy is not only the foundation to a healthy, satisfying marriage but the key to healthy families, healthy friendships, and a healthy understanding of ourselves.

The path to that joyful union starts out easy enough. We are attracted to someone and begin a process of discovering more and more about that other person. Of course, that person is doing the same thing with us. At the beginning, it is exciting and energizing. But as we grow closer, we begin to encounter fears, weaknesses, or other traits in ourselves we didn't expect.

Many people resist finding intimacy because they are frightened by the self-knowledge that will be required. Intimacy requires a "being known" that is mutual; it involves learning not only more about the other person but also more about ourselves. This rocky path of self-knowing can be enough to block many of us in our search for closeness.

Unfortunately, our culture doesn't help us in our struggle with intimacy. Early in our marriage we began to realize that our ability to love and be loved had been frustrated by some of the cultural barriers we encountered—like individualism, cynicism, and changing expectations. These cultural barriers made us defensive and afraid when we started to get closer to each other and kept us from learning how to love and accept ourselves and each other.

Cultural Barriers

1. Individualism

Our culture places a premium on individualism. We admire those who make it on their own against great odds—self-sufficient loners, like the "lonesome cowboy" or the executive at the top of the company pyramid.

Yet, although we strive for independence, we long for closeness with someone else. We hold on to a basic wish to know and be known by someone else. We want to make it on our own, but we also want to have someone standing by our side when we reach the top. In all too many cases, however, the desire for autonomy is predominant, and our desire for closeness remains a wish or a fantasy.

Intimacy asks a different question than does individualism. Intimacy asks, "Who are we?" It assumes we have already answered the question "Who am I?" and are now ready to move on to the next level of growth. But moving on involves a risk: I risk losing myself.

We experienced difficulties early in our marriage because we approached these questions differently. I was working on my "Who am I?" question by developing my career. I was busy working with high school and college students, teaching groups every week and getting a lot of affirmation and satisfaction through what I was doing. At the same time, Jan was busy working on the "Who are we?" question by focusing on our family and trying hard to make our relationship successful. She was extremely frustrated in her task by my emphasis on the "I." Interestingly, as Jan began focusing on her "Who am I?" I became more open to the "Who are we?" question. We both became freer and the closeness that resulted felt good.

Men tend to get lost in answering "Who am I?" They fear moving on to the next question. Women, however, tend to bypass the "Who am I?" question and move quickly into answering the question "Who are we?" since they attempt to develop their identities through their relationships. Healthy growth and development require that we answer these two important questions, and that we answer them in order.

Sometimes it appears that our individualism is simply a reaction to our frustration at not being able to achieve intimacy. We think we believe it when we say, "It's time for me! I want to make it on my own. I don't need anybody else." But that is not our heart talking; instead, it is usually the voice of our fears. If our heart could speak, it would share that basic desire to know and be known by another person.

2. Cynicism

Along with its high value on individualism, our culture places another barrier to intimacy before us: cynicism. We learn early not to trust the major institutions of our society. A "Bloom County" cartoon strip illustrates my point. In this particular strip, Opus, the penguin, stands under the heading, "Last Tuesday Opus was Suffering a General Crisis of Faith." Opus looks at a TV set and says, "I believe in our government." At the same time, the TV announcer is saying, "Today the president admitted sending a personally inscribed copy of Leo Buscaglia's *Living, Loving, and Learning* to Qaddafi."

Opus shakes his head, but in the next frame he says, "Well, I have faith in the forces of capitalism." But then the *Wall Street Journal* reports, "Today on Wall Street, everybody but the wiener vendors was busted."

Opus is next seen on his porch looking upward saying, "What can a fellow believe in anymore? Are there any more bastions of purity?" Then he sees a very pregnant woman approaching. Running down to her, he leans against her and says, "Ah . . . motherhood!" The pregnant woman looks down and says, "Surrogate."

What little faith we may have in our culture is up for grabs. Our confidence in government and the other "stable" institutions has been eroded. With one out of two marriages ending in divorce, that "stable" institution also appears to be quite shaky.

Unfortunately, many people start out marriage with either a fear or an anticipation of dissolution. The terms of the divorce are worked out with the prenuptial agreements. That kind of cynicism provides a poor foundation for building the kind of trust necessary to the development of an intimate relationship. Caryl Avery, a freelance writer who specializes in health and psychology, recently said in an article in *Psychology Today:* "People who have successfully built an intimate relationship know its power and comfort. But they also know that taking the emotional risks that allow intimacy to happen isn't easy. Preconditioned on the sharing of feelings, intimacy requires consummate trust. And today trust is in short supply."[1]

Despite the statistics and cynicism of our age, marriage has yet to fall into disfavor. Statistics show that over 95 percent of persons will marry and over 80 percent of the men who are either widowed or divorced will remarry. The percentage of women who will remarry is just a little less than the 80 percent mark.[2]

Divorce may be a common experience today, but those divorcing are not giving up on the idea of marriage or the need for closeness. "They hope to find a new love," says author Judith Wallerstein in the book *Second Chances,* "a more enriching relationship, a more responsive sexual partner, a more supportive companion, a better provider."[3]

3. Changing Expectations

Today, we look at a healthy relationship as the precursor to marriage. Only two people are closely concerned with the marriage process today: the bride and the groom. Parents and other family members are only peripheral to the process, except for maybe paying for the wedding. The church may play a part or it may not. The state issues a license and has laws about common property. But the prospective bride and groom determine what is to happen, and, for them, love is the primary prerequisit for intimacy.

In the not-too-long-ago past, a very different situation existed. The feelings of love were in many cases either a minimal issue or an absent one. Parents and other members of the family, the church, the community, and other local customs often competed with each other to see who would have the major influence in bringing two people together. Intimacy or emotional closeness was not considered a necessary prerequisite for marriage.

The conflict between the generations in the play *Fiddler on the Roof* portrayed this. Tevye, the father, didn't understand this thing called love, which was so important to his daughters. To him, the past was good enough. "Tradition!" That was all that mattered. The family took great interest in who was being married. They worked with the matchmaker to consider the benefits not only to their daughter, but to the whole family. If the daughter would just marry the butcher, for instance, she, and probably the whole family, would always have meat to eat.

Money was also a primary concern—not that the parents were mercenary. But the marrying off of children was part of the economy of the family. Marrying for love was frivolous, especially when marrying the right person could help the family survive. We some-times forget that we are not far removed in time from a society that depended on the land for its livelihood. In that time, these matters were of greater concern in a marriage than were matters of love and intimacy. Our more industrial and affluent society provides greater options in relationships, including the fulfill-ment of the desire for love and closeness.

So we are caught. We have basic fears about getting close to each other. These fears are compounded by the changes in our culture and society. The old ex-pectations that often helped hold people together are fading, and nothing seems to be taking their place. No wonder we are afraid to confront head-on the issue of intimacy.

Personal Barriers

Even after we understood how those cultural barri-ers were affecting our marriage, we were unable to be close to each other. We sensed there were other barri-ers to intimacy we hadn't identified.

Recently, we listened to a tape of a man speaking to adolescents about the barriers to closeness young people encounter in their relationships. "The biggest barrier to intimacy," he said, "is selfishness." Then he added, "Selfishness is the opposite of love."

Now that didn't fit our definition of love, so we struggled for some time with what he had said. We'd always believed that the opposite of love is fear. If love is perfect when fear is absent, as the apostle John says, then love and fear are at the opposite ends of the continuum. We hadn't thought about selfishness and how that fit in.

Then we thought about our own marriage. For

years, we have struggled to develop closeness in our marriage. We knew we wanted to experience greater intimacy, but we couldn't seem to break out of the patterns in which we were caught. We would start to get close, then something would happen that would set one of us off and we would distance ourselves from each other. As that distancing wore thin, we would kind of gloss things over and make up. Did we become distant because we were selfish or self-centered?

The more we debated his idea, the more we came to believe that the speaker was at least on the right track. Perhaps selfishness is the opposite of love. People who think only of themselves are so busy trying to maintain some fragile sense of who they are, that they don't have the time or energy to think about anyone else.

But is our problem with intimacy caused by our selfishness? If it is, how does knowing that help us relate better? Do we just stop being self-centered? If we tell people to just be less selfish, can they do it? We didn't think so.

The truth is, if someone had come up to us a couple of years ago and said that the problems we were experiencing in our marriage were because of our selfishness, it wouldn't have helped us much. Most people we talk with have been told a number of times what's wrong in their relationship. They know the formulas for fixing relationships, yet they remain stuck in patterns that deny them the closeness they desire.

As we continued to think about what that speaker had said, we were convinced that something was missing—a piece of the intimacy puzzle that we somehow don't connect to the issue of intimacy and, therefore, completely overlook. Something must happen on a deeper level that trips us up just as we get started and keeps us stuck in patterns we cannot break.

We were talking about this as we prepared for a weekend retreat, and we asked each other what were some of the things we wished we had known early in our marriage that we know now? The result of that conversation, and many weekend retreats and seminars, provide the basis of what we want to say to you in this book. Our wish list formed those missing pieces that were necessary for true intimacy.

We wished we had known more about how our personalities were attracted to each other and what weaknesses were based on those underlying attractions. We've since discovered that the parts of our personalities that drew us to each other included a dark side, a side that can be very unattractive unless we can understand the whole picture. We'll talk about how our personalities affect our ability to love and be loved in Part Two of this book.

We wished we had known more about how our family backgrounds contributed to our needs and expectations of each other. We share a lot of what we have learned about how our backgrounds shape not only our behaviors, but especially our expectations. We'll look at how the past affects our ability to love and be loved in Part Three.

Our personalities and our pasts: these, we believe, are two of the factors that hindered intimacy in our relationship—not selfishness. And behind each of these elements is fear. We're afraid of our differences. And we're afraid of things that have hurt us in the past so we stay away from them, or react as we did so long ago to protect ourselves from being hurt. Our personalities, our pasts, and our fears are the hidden factors that keep us from being partners in intimacy. Once we have dealt with these factors, we can begin to look at the positive ingredients that go into developing a healthy relationship.

The only advice I remember getting before we were married came out of our meeting with the dean of men at the college we were attending. I remember him looking at me and saying, "Dave, don't ever stop being polite to Jan. Remember to open the car door for her." For over thirty-five years I've followed that advice—but I wish I'd had more help back in those early days. Part Four of this book will give you the building blocks of a loving relationship, which have helped us—and the hundreds of couples we've counseled—develop intimacy in marriage.

As we struggle with these questions we need to recognize that intimacy is a delicate issue that consumes much of our energy. Many of us spend a lot of time thinking about it, searching for it, and longing for it. Other couples spend a lot of time and energy denying any interest in intimacy, saying they don't need it or want it. The truth is that all of us long for intimacy, but most of us are simply afraid of it.

Behind our fears and frustrations about the subject of intimacy lies a basic fact: We have been created for relationships, and unless we can learn how to build, maintain, and enjoy intimate relationships, we are always going to be haunted by a sense of longing and emptiness.

We share with you in this book what we have shared with many others over the recent years. We trust it will provide some concrete information that you can use to become partners in intimacy.

A Starting Point

If you are ready to begin to set aside your preconceived ideas about what keeps you from finding the closeness you want, then read on. In order to overcome our fears and break out of our frustrating patterns, we need to take off our masks and see ourselves on a deeper level, where there has been woundedness and damage that has been left unrepaired, unresolved, and even ignored.

A journey into that area of ourselves is risky and painful. It will require that we look more closely at ourselves, at our personalities, and at our basic fears. But first, let's take a moment to dismiss some of the myths we attach to the subject of intimacy. These also keep us from finding the closeness we want in our marriage relationship.

2

Nine Myths About Intimacy

WHEN JAN AND I were dating, I had a real problem with jealousy. My insecurities flared whenever Jan spent too much time with anyone, even her college roommate. Obviously, we had some pretty intense discussions about my concerns and Jan's feelings of being boxed in.

The strangest thing happened. Soon after we were married my jealousy problem was cured. After some months of this noticeable shift in my behavior, Jan asked me what had changed. I told her, "Well, you're mine now that we're married. I don't have to worry about anyone else taking you away from me." Needless to say, my idea of "owning her" did not feel very good to her. In fact, that conversation produced a change in her attitude. Her insecurities were stirred up, and *she* started being jealous for the first time. For some time, I couldn't understand what she was experiencing. The problem was that we had different beliefs about marriage—some of them untruths or myths. The myth I held on to was that once we were married, we "owned" each other. Jan's myth was that somehow her husband's love would make her feel secure forever after.

What do you believe about the subject of intimacy? What were you taught? These beliefs often keep us stuck where we are. Take a moment to assess your beliefs about relationships. Read each of the following statements and decide which are true and which are false.

An Intimacy Checklist

1. If the other person really loves me, he/she will always know what I want or need to be happy.

True _____   False _____

2. The best indicator of a good marriage is a good sex life.

True _____   False _____

3. The level of satisfaction and intimacy automatically increases over the years of the relationship.

True _____   False _____

4. It doesn't matter how I behave, the other person should show love for me simply because we are married to each other.

True _____   False _____

5. If we are really close, we should be able to point out each other's errors and shortcomings without feeling threatened.

True _____   False _____

6. My spouse either loves me or doesn't; if not, there is nothing I can do to make it any different.

True _____   False _____

7. The more we can disclose—both good and bad information—to each other, the closer we become.

True _____   False _____

8. Keeping the feelings of romantic love alive is necessary to fuel an intimate relationship.

True _____   False _____

9. I have to feel love toward the other person before I can help the relationship become closer.

True _____   False _____

How did you answer? Did you answer true to any of the statements? If you answered false to every statement, your beliefs about intimacy are accurate. Each of the above statements is a myth.

MYTH #1: Intimacy Is Being Able to Read Each Other's Mind

The desire to have the other person read our mind is really an extension of one of the wishes we had as a child, but it seems an innocent enough goal to have in a marriage. As children, we subconsciously longed to return to that wonderful state within the womb where everything was taken care of automatically. Now we think, *The person I love will know what I need and provide it for me even before I know I need it.*

This myth finds some positive reinforcement in the early stages of a relationship. As we are getting to know someone new, the other person can read us and know what we need at some given moment. And as that person responds to our need, our wish is being fulfilled. This gives support to the wish, and so we wish all the more for this automatic fulfillment to take place. In the early stages of a relationship, we are still far enough away from each other emotionally that we are able to see needs and respond without fear. As we get closer to each other, we find that our own fears about closeness get stirred up and blind us to the needs of the other person.

One of the most common expressions of this myth is the statement, "It isn't the same if I have to ask for it."

"If I have to tell you what I need or want," we say, "then somehow our relationship is lacking closeness, and I am disappointed by you. And if I have to ask you for what I want or need, it spoils it for me, so in many cases I would rather do without than ask."

Mary struggled with this. She was about to end her marriage with Tom because she was not willing to give up this myth. They had long, heated discussions about Tom's failure to anticipate Mary's needs. "If you can't anticipate what I need, then we aren't as close as I thought we were, and I'm not interested in being with you anymore."

Tom's response was one of frustration and help-lessness. "I still do the nice things for her that I've always done," he said, "but she's gotten to where she simply expects me to do them, and they don't count anymore. I don't know what to do. I love her, but she doesn't believe me anymore. If I do something for her after she tells me, it causes worse problems than when I don't do it."

Myth #1 has become a barrier to the love and close-ness Mary and Tom long for. They need to learn that no one can know what we need or want unless we tell him.

MYTH #2: Sex Is Intimacy and Intimacy Is Sex

Physical intimacy and emotional intimacy are two different things. You can have intimacy without sex just as you can have sex without emotional intimacy. Yet many people still see the two as the same thing. In fact, we sometimes substitute sex for emotional intimacy without really knowing the difference.

Many times we believe this myth because we are afraid of affection. Affection makes us feel vulnerable, and when we feel vulnerable, we become afraid (there's that old barrier to intimacy again—fear). We may be afraid of vulnerability because we experienced it as a dangerous thing while we were growing up. Perhaps someone, even a parent, knew something personal about us, and used it to embarrass or somehow control us.

The person who holds on to this myth feels reassured when the emotional aspects of a relationship are under stress that the relationship is stable if the couple has sex together. The husband or wife believing this myth wants to have sex after an argument in order to feel okay about the marriage. A more serious example is the partner who fears affection and vulnerability and, thus, uses sex to fulfill all of his or her emotional needs. Bill did this.

His major concern in his relationship with his wife was that their sex life had dwindled over the past years. "What's the national average for a married couple?" he asked me in front of his wife, Sue. Before I could answer, he answered his own question. "Two or three times a week! We're lucky if we can have sex once a month. In fact, I doubt if it's even that often."

Bill and Sue had been married only four years, and he foresaw a bleak future for their marriage. He had the statistics, he used Bible verses, he quoted previous counselors, and he even knew the average for the people in his office.

Sue finally spoke up in her own defense, saying that she was tired of simply being a sex object to Bill. She continued quickly before he could jump in and defend himself. "He wants to make love to me and then act like everything is okay. Then he's nice for a day, but he quickly gets mad if we don't have sex again. I'm tired of trying to appease him with sex. I want more out of our marriage than that."

As we talked, it was clear that Bill equated closeness with sex. In fact, he really didn't understand the distinction Sue was trying to make. "Sue told me it would help if I would just hold her without it leading to sex. I tried that, but it was never enough. She just used that to avoid sex," Bill said in his defense. "Now I guess I just ignore her most of the time. It's too painful otherwise. I mean, what's a man to do?"

Well, to start, Bill needed to give up the myth and begin to see sex as a response to closeness, not as a means to closeness.

MYTH #3: Intimacy Will Grow Automatically Once It's Started

There is nothing automatic about intimacy. It takes a lot of work. We are led into a false sense of security because the movement toward intimacy seems so easy in the early stages of a relationship. If you can picture the emotional distance between two people when they first meet, it would look something like this:

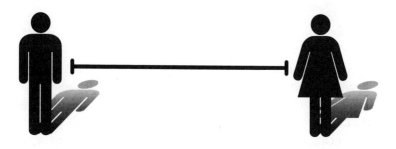

At the beginning of a relationship, when the emotional distance between the couple is fairly wide, movement closer is easy. But as the distance between the two decreases emotionally, the risk of being known and the risk of being abandoned or smothered —and all of the fears associated with those risks—get stirred up and one or both partners want to run away. They can only get comfortable again by distancing themselves from one another. Two common, unsatisfying relationships develop: the pursuer-pursued cycle and the emotional blowup cycle.

The Pursuer–Pursued Cycle

In the pursuer-pursued cycle, one person wants more intimacy and "pursues" the other person in order to attain that closeness. At the same time, the other person (the pursued) feels the increased pressure and begins to back away from the relationship. But the pursued will back away only so far, because the fear of being abandoned kicks in. This relationship looks something like this:

Some couples develop this style of relating to the point where they can switch roles. The pursued suddenly stops, turns around, and starts pursuing, like this:

Almost as if on cue, the former pursuer begins to back away and becomes the pursued. Jan and I switched roles when we were first married, as we mentioned. I had been jealous when we were courting—I was the pursuer—but once we were married Jan became jealous of my time—she became the pursuer.

This is a "dance" couples perform. The rules of the dance require that the couple never get beyond a certain point in emotional closeness. It's as if they have a pole tied to their waists and they always stay at a predetermined distance from each other emotionally. The pole keeps them from getting either too close or too far away from each other.

The Emotional Blowup Cycle

Another style is when two people continue to move closer to each other, but as the distance between them decreases, the emotions "heat up" and one of the persons unconsciously creates a problem that leads to an emotional outburst, which pushes the couple apart. The sequence could be described like this:

You can imagine that this becomes increasingly frustrating. Usually, a couple will finally settle on some degree of emotional distance; this prevents further explosions but ends up being very unsatisfying. One woman said, "I'm afraid to spend too much time with my husband. If we get too close, either he picks a fight or I do." Some couples, however, continue this routine of moving closer, exploding, and then moving apart even after they have divorced and remarried someone else.

Couples who are building healthy relationships practice a variant of this last "dance." Instead of the explosion and the subsequent distancing, these couples find ways to resolve their conflict and to continue the building process. Healthy relationships follow a pattern of "waves and troughs," but with a somewhat steady overall increase in intimacy. You could chart it something like this:

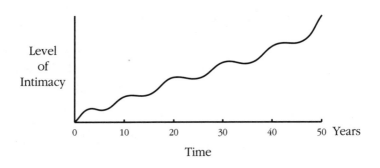

MYTH #4: Love and Behavior Are Not Related

Often we assume that the other person can love us unconditionally. Marge was raised by a mother who constantly criticized Marge and her father. The whole time her mother was doing this, she was also affirming verbally how much she loved both her husband and her daughter. Over the years, Marge learned to filter out the criticism and focus only on the loving behaviors of her mother. "It doesn't matter what she says to me, I know she loves me."

Marge's husband, Ray, couldn't stand to be around Marge's mother, especially if any of her other family members were present. "I can't see how Marge can just overlook her mother's criticism. I think it's cruel and abusive. And now Marge is doing the same thing with me. I won't put up with it! If you can't help her, I'm out of here."

Marge sat there with a puzzled look on her face. "I don't see why he's so sensitive. He knows I love him. I wish you could help him." Marge accepted the myth that all that mattered in her relationship with Ray was that she loved him. She honestly could not understand why he was so sensitive.

Believing this myth is similar to believing the lie "sticks and stones will break my bones, but names will never hurt me." Many of us were taught this lie as children. We shouted those words at the bully, but it didn't really help then, and it doesn't help now. Names and words can wound us deeply.

Often we minimize criticism from a parent in order to hold on to the idea that that parent loved us. If we were to validate our experience of harshness and criticism, we would have difficulty believing that parent loved us. Since the injury took place when we were children, often when we were preschool age, logic and rationality were meaningless concepts to us at that age. So when we try to reason ourselves out of this myth, we must recognize that we are arguing with a part of ourselves that doesn't respond to reason.

Somehow, we need to see that when our behavior and our words do not match, we are giving a double message; usually, most people will hold on to the negative part of that message. Behavior does count, and so do the words we say. Love and behavior are related.

MYTH #5: People Who Love Each Other Can Accept Constructive Criticism

Being close does not mean we can begin the task of fixing the other person. This myth is a cousin to the previous one, but it focuses primarily on the area of "constructive" criticism. This is a myth because it works directly against intimacy.

(As two people become closer emotionally, one of the big fears that begins to stir within them is the fear that once you really get to know me, you will not like me and will leave me. When one partner begins to try to help the other with "constructive" criticism, pointing out the other person's shortcomings or correcting his or her errors, the very thing we fear in a relationship is beginning to happen. The other person is noticing parts of me that he or she does not like. No one can experience this without becoming either angry or defensive or both.⟩

You may protest that you are only trying to be helpful. However, unless the other person experiences the "constructive" criticism as helpful, it is not helpful. We often try to "help" in this way to take attention away from our own faults. We are unconsciously thinking, "If I can begin to help you improve yourself, maybe you won't notice the things that I need to improve in myself. As long as I can keep the focus on you, I'm off the hook." The one exception may be when the person has asked for the constructive help—maybe!

Over the years, my wife has been my best critic whenever I am speaking to a group. Many years ago I asked her to tell me what she thought about what I said and how I said it. Sometimes it was difficult for me to listen to what she offered, but since I really wanted to know what she had to say, it seldom was a barrier to our becoming closer. I say "seldom" because sometimes the constructive criticism was more than I wanted, and I reacted defensively. There is no room in any relationship for unrequested criticism, even if it is meant to be "constructive."

MYTH #6: Someone Either Loves Me or Not—And That's That!

This statement is one of the favorites of our day. I can't count the number of times someone has said to me, "I don't know why we're coming to counseling. I don't love him/her anymore, and there's nothing anyone can do about that. It's over!" Sometimes these people will work very hard to soften what they are saying. They will try to make the distinction between "loving" and "being in love." Rich had told me he still loved Kathy, but it was the kind of love he might have had for his sister. "I'm no longer 'in love' with her," he added emphatically. My standard response to these statements is "That's okay. It's not really an issue anyway."

Before I lose the couple's attention, I go on to ask, "How long has it been since either of you has behaved in a loving way to the other person?" Usually they say that it has been some time since anything like that has happened. No wonder the feelings of love have vanished.

Feelings of love usually wither and dry up in a sterile, dry environment. Love needs to be nurtured and fed. And when loving behaviors start to take place without pressure, the feelings of love are often rekindled.

When I explained these ideas to Rich, he thought for a while and then agreed to test my hypothesis. He and Kathy had been separated for more than six months by the time they came to see me, and they were starting to think about taking the next step toward divorce. But they had been married more than twenty-six years and felt they owed it to themselves and their family to talk to someone.

Rich and Kathy decided to test my theory over the next six months, so they started spending more time together. They were careful not to pressure each other, and they backed off when one of them felt unable to move ahead in their relationship. They also focused on doing caring things for each other.

As our sessions approached the one-year mark, it was obvious that there was not going to be a divorce. I asked Rich what he was feeling in the way of love. "It's not what I want it to be, but Kathy is more than a sister to me. I think you might be right."

The feelings of love can come back if they are nurtured by the behaviors of love.

MYTH #7: Knowing Everything About the Other Person Is an Essential Part of Intimacy

Honesty is a basic ingredient for intimacy. But we sometimes confuse honesty with knowing everything possible about the other person and revealing everything about ourselves. It is a myth that intimacy results from "telling everything," or being totally open. Our spouse may not be able to handle some of what we may disclose. Other times, our total disclosure of ourselves destroys the "mystery of personhood" that is so important to any intimate relationship.

What about when one partner betrays the other partner, as in having an affair? How much information is enough? Before we answer that question, we need to answer some other questions. Why, if we have been unfaithful, do we want to disclose this information? Are we seeking to be punished in order not to feel so guilty? Or why do we, if we have been betrayed, want to know everything the other person did? Will it really help in rebuilding the relationship? You can see that complex issues are involved here. Our efforts at knowing all about the other person, especially in this case, may not help us in our search for intimacy.

Bryan and Jill came to see me because Jill had had an affair. Initially, Bryan had no idea about what was going on; he only knew that something was wrong with the marriage. The couple had previously been to another counselor who, promoting total openness, asserted that Jill had to tell Bryan everything. Feeling guilty, Jill blurted out what had been going on and then collapsed in tears. Then, the counselor encouraged Jill to continue talking, sharing with Bryan every detail she could remember. He complimented Bryan for his forgiving spirit as Bryan listened to the entire confession. Jill and Bryan saw the counselor a few more times and felt their problem was resolved. Jill had confessed, and Bryan had forgiven.

That was over a year before they consulted me. Jill said that all was nice for about three months, and then Bryan started asking her for more details about the affair. Sometimes she told Bryan a little; at other times she insisted there was nothing else to say and she didn't want to talk about it. It didn't matter what she said or did, Bryan wasn't satisfied. He became obsessed with knowing more about what had happened, and now their problems went beyond the affair.

Bryan had found out the name of the other man during their earlier counseling sessions, so about six months before they came to see me, Bryan contacted him and pressured him into giving him some additional details. Bryan was convinced that if he could find out enough details he would understand why his wife had done this awful thing. But the more he found out, the more obsessed he was with knowing more, all in the name of "total knowing" or complete openness.

The couple's relationship deteriorated beyond anything they could have imagined. According to Jill, Bryan was always angry with her. Bryan countered with the fact that he couldn't trust her because she wouldn't be totally open with him. The more Bryan pressed, the more Jill withdrew. Their marriage was hanging together by a thin thread that seemed ready to break at any moment.

A moratorium had to be declared for Bryan and Jill to have any chance of healing in their relationship. It took some time to convince Bryan that he had more information than he knew how to handle and that any more information would only add more hurt, which he would eventually have to get over. It's been touch and go for some time, but as they spend time together and focus on where they are headed, they appear to be building some trust back into their relationship.

It's hard to know where to draw the line on full disclosure. The most important guideline you should use is to ask yourself, "Why do I want to know or share this information? What is the primary motivation?" If it's some principle of openness, or fully knowing each other—"We're going to be 100 percent honest in this relationship no matter what"—or a need to clear your own conscience at the other's expense, you'd better think again. Yes, we are to speak the truth, but it should always be tempered by love. Sometimes the total truth will destroy a relationship. Your partner may be like Bryan, who was haunted by the knowledge of Jill's relationship with another man. The ultimate test should be to ask yourself, "Will sharing this information build a greater sense of intimacy?" If not, total openness may not be appropriate.

MYTH #8: Romantic Love Is Essential for Intimacy

Many people realize this is a myth, but they still are governed by it. Many of the books we read and the TV programs and movies we watch reinforce this myth. Yet the expectation that romantic love can and should sustain a true and satisfying intimate relationship puts an incredible strain on marriages in our culture today.

Romantic love has been described as sweaty palms, heart palpitations, obsessive thinking, and the belief that this relationship will meet all of our dreams. Think about the dichotomies in statements like "falling head over heels in love" and "I was swept off my feet." These are wonderful feelings, but no one can maintain these feelings over the years.

It's important to note here that we are not talking about romance and doing romantic things with each other. Loving interaction, as we will see later in the book, is an important ingredient in the building of closeness. But the idea that these romantic feelings can be sustained and can provide a foundation for an intimate marriage puts a strain on the relationship to the point where it undermines, rather than supports, intimacy.

Although the notion of romantic love can be dated at least as far back as the Song of Solomon in the Bible, our acceptance of it as an ideal goes back only about 800 years. Sometime during the late twelfth or early thirteenth century, Eleanor of Aquitaine and her daughter, the Countess Marie of Champagne, summoned a cleric, Andreas, to their palace at Poitiers and instructed him to prepare a manual on courtly love. The chaplain's book, *The Art of Courtly Love,* still influences the way men and women relate to each other.

One of Andreas's statements in his book gives a taste of the problem he created:

> We declare and we hold as firmly established that love cannot exert its powers between two people who are married to each other. For lovers give each other everything freely, under no compulsion of necessity, but married people are in duty bound to give in to each other's desires and deny themselves to each other in nothing.

Andreas's work was not written to describe marriage relationships. In fact, his book was designed to describe "courtly" love, illicit relationships between people in the promiscuous court of Aquitaine.

Andreas laid the foundation for the idealization of women, the importance of gentlemanly courtesy, and the emphasis on potent emotions, along with a sense of eternal oneness, undying devotion, and ecstasy. The part of his work we no longer give credibility to in our daily lives is the "agony of a love that is unfulfilled." Andreas taught that for love to be "true" love, it had to be incomplete. While two people might be passionately in love, their prior commitments to their marital partners precluded them from ever acting upon this love. Their love was expressed at a distance and was idealized; romantic love could be maintained only by distance.

The writings of Keats, Dante, and Shakespeare; the operas of Wagner; and movies like *Gone with the Wind* and *Love Story* have all shown the impact of Andreas's work. Our desire to marry out of passion is an expression of his thought, but we have contaminated his work by believing that this passion can be maintained throughout marriage. In the long run, however, intimacy and closeness are related to romance, but really have little to do with the idea of romantic love.

MYTH #9: The Relationship Can Grow Only When We Feel Good About Each Other

Again, the opposite of this statement is true. A relationship will grow only as we are able to learn to work through those times when we really don't feel like doing the things that make relationships work. One of the popular songs of not too long ago said, "Loving you is easy because you're beautiful." There is no verse on what to do "when loving you is difficult because right now you look ugly to me or I feel ugly." But that's when healthy relationships really get to work.

There are two important aspects to love. One is the feeling and emotion of love. The second aspect to love goes beyond feelings and emotions to commitment: Love is also a decision.

When Jesus told His disciples that He was giving them a new commandment, "Love each other as I have loved you," He was not talking about a feeling or an emotion. You cannot demand feelings or emotions. But you can demand a decision.

When someone says he or she no longer loves another person, I often ask when he or she decided to stop loving that person. Usually there was a point at which that decision was made. That decision can be reversed, and that's where the commitment part of love comes into focus. Commitment keeps us doing the behaviors of love even when we don't feel like it. And when we act this way, the feelings and emotions of love can and do return.

These myths about intimacy all work as barriers to our finding the closeness we really long for. As you've read through this chapter it may appear to be very clear that these are in fact myths. But they still attract us. In order to break the hold the myths may still have on us, we need to understand how our personalities affect our ability to love and be loved which we will discuss in the second part of this book. Before we begin, let us give you an idea of what we will be doing in that section.

Learning the Differences in Our Personalities and How to Love Them

People are different; we all know that for a fact. But in our marriages, we often struggle with our differences. At the beginning of a relationship, the differences are attractive. We see something in the other person that we like, or we see that the other person is comfortable with something we are uncomfortable with in ourselves. It isn't too long after the wedding, however, that each one begins to work on the other, attempting to change the other. And then the sparks begin to fly! We usually believe that things would be smoother and easier if that other person were more like us.

One of the major variables we bring to our marriage relationship is our personality. How we understand that personality is part of the problem. We often interpret the other person's behavior in the light of our own personality. We think he or she should see what we see, think the way we think, and understand things as we understand them. For example, before we were married, Jan looked at me and saw a quiet reserve that intrigued her. I appeared to "have it all together." I looked at her ability to relate easily with other people and was convinced that nothing could stop her. She could do anything! We were attracted to our opposites.

After the wedding Jan found out that my quiet, mysterious reserve was irritating, even morbid at times. I needed to be more outgoing—like her. I found that her ease with other people became very draining. Why couldn't she be more content to be alone—like me?

After the irritating phase of seeing our differences, we moved on to taking them personally. I thought, *Jan could care less about my needs—all she wants to do is be with people. Why is she doing that to me?* Jan looked at my quietness and felt as if I didn't care anymore. I was retreating from her. She thought, *Why is he so anti-social? He needs to be with people more!*

Now two persons don't have to be opposites to experience this conflict. Neither one of us is very organized. It became easy to project our own weakness —lack of organization—onto the other person and criticize him or her for that lack. We don't like seeing in our spouse the weakness we are trying to deny within ourselves.

What we found out some years later was that each of us was acting according to his or her personality. There was nothing personal against the other person in our behavior. It took a test to help us understand how our differences affected us. The Myers-Briggs Type Indicator®, or the MBTI®* is a descriptive test based on the observations of Carl Jung, a Swiss psychiatrist, that defines eight basic personality traits that will affect us in our relationships. Over the years we have found that understanding these traits is most helpful in accepting the differences between people.

The interesting thing about this test is that you cannot get a bad score, since all persons have all eight traits in their personality. The eight traits form four pairs of opposites, and each of us prefers to use one pair over the other. The quiz at the beginning of each of the next four chapters will help you identify the four traits you use the most. The combinations of the four traits lead to sixteen basic personality styles, within which we still have an infinite variety of personalities. The eight personality traits are listed below:

- Extravert or introvert
- Sensing or intuitive
- Thinking or feeling
- Judging or perceiving

These traits are believed to be inherited from our families. Often we are a combination of our parents' dominant traits. Sometimes we are like a grandparent. We don't learn the trait from our families or from the environment, although our families can either confirm our traits or create an internal conflict with our traits. They are as natural to us as the color of our eyes. Therefore, the goal is not to change what we are, but to understand ourselves better and to accept the way we are. In fact, when we try to block out a trait or change it because it hasn't been valued, say, within

* MBTI and Myers-Briggs Type Indicator are registered trademarks of Consulting Psychologists Press, Inc., Palo Alto, California.

our families, we will experience a lot of inner conflict and insecurity, much like what happens when we try to make left-handed children right-handed.

Part Two will introduce each pair of traits with a short quiz and then discuss the characteristics of each trait and how the different personality types interact with one another in a relationship. Relax. There are no incompatible combinations, but each couple will have their own unique set of "adjustments" to make. As you begin each chapter, take the time to answer the questions in the quiz. Base your answers on how you are usually, not how you wish you could be or think you should be.

Remember, the goal of this next section is to help each of us better understand our own strengths and weaknesses as well as the strengths and weaknesses of our spouses. As we understand these traits better, we will find that the other person's behavior will not be as threatening to us as it may have been. So when I hear Jan "thinking out loud" I don't have to feel it as pressure. In the same way, Jan can remind herself that my quietness is not rejection; it is just a part of my personality. Instead of trying to change each other into what we think the other should be, we can celebrate the differences, for every intimate relationship is drawn together as much by the differences as by the similarities.

PART TWO

How Our Personalities Affect Our Ability to Love and Be Loved

3

Extravert
or Introvert
Relator?

NOT TOO LONG AGO, our son participated in an outreach program to Mexico. The group he was with went on their own bus and camped out along the way until they got to their destination. They were there for several months. On their way home, our son called and asked if the group could come by our house, four or five at a time, to take showers. They were coming through our area, and they were scheduled to camp out in a church that had offered its facilities. Apparently, there were no showers there, and the group hadn't had any place to clean up for several days, so they were desperate.

After trying to shuttle a few persons at a time, back and forth from the church where the bus was parked, Jan told our son, "This is too much trouble. Just bring the bus on over with everyone." All thirty-seven of them came, and while they waited their turn for the shower, they laid around the family room, watching TV and talking, and Jan started baking chocolate chip cookies for everyone.

About that time, I came home. "Where did all these people come from?" I asked rather incredulously. I hadn't seen our son yet, but had some idea that this group had something to do with him.

"Isn't this great?" Jan responded. "What a privilege to have them all here and hear their stories!"

I was thinking, *Great?* I had been looking forward to coming home to a nice quiet house, reading the newspaper, and maybe going to bed early. *How can Jan think this is great when it's chaos to me?* I wondered.

Jan was in her glory as she helped the leaders cook up a big pot of spaghetti to go with her cookies. I stayed on the fringe and watched. After a while, I gradually entered into the festive evening, but was relieved to learn they were still sleeping at the church that night.

I can't understand why, but Jan loves it when people crowd into the downstairs of our house, some talking to her in the kitchen as she cooks, and everyone laughing and enjoying themselves. And Jan can't understand why I get so quiet in that kind of situation.

Perhaps you identify with me in this story. If so, you are probably an introvert. Or maybe you identify more with Jan. If so, you are probably an extravert. Circle the letter, in the short quiz below, that indicates how you would react in a situation similar to the one described.

Are You an Extravert or an Introvert?

1. You have been invited to a party and you know only the host and the hostess. You are obligated to go. While you are there, will you tend either to:

A. Find it stimulating to meet new and interesting people and enjoy talking to this group or that group?

B. Find someone who is interested in something you are interested in and spend most of the evening talking with one person at a time?

2. Your hostess has planned several games for everyone to play. You've never heard of the first game. Do you tend to:

A. Decide to play the game in order to understand it?
B. Want to let others play first so you can watch in order to understand the game?

3. On the way home you realize that it has been a pleasant evening. Do you tend to:

A. Find that you have renewed energy and are keyed up because of the stimulating evening?
B. Find that, in spite of the enjoyment of the evening, you are tired and feel drained?

4. You've had a very tiring day. When you come home in the evening, do you usually tend to:

A. Want to call a friend or two and meet for dinner?
B. Take the phone off the hook so you can have a quiet evening alone?

5. If something enters your mind, would others say that you usually tend to:

A. Say it almost immediately?
B. Think about it before you talk about it?

6. If there is a long pause in a conversation, do you:

A. Feel as if you should fill the silence by saying something?
B. Hardly notice the pause at all or find it refreshing?

7. Do you enjoy working:

A. With lots of people around you?
B. Alone so that there is little interruption?

8. When you were a child, did you:

A. Need to have lots of friends around?
B. Tend to be quite happy playing alone?

9. Do you tend to:

A. Jump right in when faced with a new challenge?
B. Stand back and check out a new situation before you commit?

How did you score? More A's than B's? If so, you are the extravert personality. You're like Jan. If you scored more B's than A's, you are the introvert personality. You're more like me.

We will all have some of both traits, but one trait will dominate. It's like being right-handed or left-handed. Most of us have both hands, but one hand dominates; we depend on it the most to accomplish the tasks of life. In the same way, we all are somewhat of an extravert and somewhat of an introvert, but one of these traits dominates. That's the trait you need to write in the space below:

I am an _____.

In our marriage seminars on intimacy, I always say that the extravert is someone who is always thinking out loud. "There's a greased slide from your brain to your mouth," I say to Jan. "If it enters your mind, you say it."

Jan, who is the extravert, comes back with, "What's wrong with being so quick? It's much better than being like you. You have a French horn in your head. I give you a little information—and then I have to sit and wait and wait. It takes so long for that information to go around and around all those winding passages. Eventually, it comes out the other end. Or gets stuck in there someplace. I get so tired waiting for a response from you."

A short definition of the extravert might be "someone who thinks out loud." They work things out as they talk. The introvert is someone who thinks before he or she speaks; the introvert has to process the information before saying something.

It helps to think of these terms as answering the question "How do I process information?" The extravert processes immediately. The introvert processes more slowly. Jan says I process and process and process.

The introvert often appears to be slow compared to

the extravert, but I have to remind Jan that I am processing.

We always tell partners who are extraverts, like Jan, to wait for the introverts to complete this process. If they dash ahead with more information before the introverts have responded, the introvert will become very confused.

"You see," I explain, "I have to go back in and run the new information through the French horn again."

The interaction that usually takes place between an extravert and an introvert revolves around this processing cycle. Extraverts process information by talking, and introverts process before talking. When Jan is processing out loud, it feels like a lot of pressure to me. I don't know what her bottom line is, so I assume she means everything as bottom line. Our culture has a word for that: *nagging.*

On the other hand, while she is talking out loud, I am processing what she is saying within me, so I am not talking. In fact, the more she talks the more I have to process and the less I will talk. Soon she forgets that I am processing, and a bigger, more hurtful word comes into play: *rejection.* When I don't respond, Jan feels that I don't care.

We've watched couples in this complicated dance. The extravert will talk and then pause, waiting for a response. The problem is that the introvert has a ten-second processing cycle, but the extravert has only an eight-second tolerance for silence. Just as the introvert is starting to talk, the extravert starts talking again and the introvert has to go back inside to process all of the new information.

You can see the frustration of such a cycle. The extravert talks and talks while the introvert processes and processes, but the introvert never has enough time to start talking before the extravert finally gives up, hurt and angry. Now the introvert has the time to start talking, but it is too late. Over the years, this becomes a pattern of nagging and rejection. Unfortunately, we don't recognize that the roots of that pattern are not based on nagging and rejection but on subtle and initially attractive differences in personality.

Another way to think of the terms *extravert* and *introvert* is to see them as answering this question: Which world do I relate to? The outer world of people? Or the inner would of ideas?

Extraverts and introverts are equally likely to be male or female. And remember, no one is only an extravert or an introvert, although each of us develops one attitude over the other as our dominant inclination.

In the American culture, there are three extraverts for each introvert.[1] As a result, there is a lot of pressure in our society to be an extravert. In business, in social settings, and in other places, we admire the extravert's ability to take an active posture. So if we are introverted, we often grow up envying the extravert and put a lot of pressure on ourselves to be that way.

The Worlds of the Extravert and the Introvert

As an extravert, Jan needs to think out loud. Her extraverted talking often includes the animated use of her hands. She processes her thoughts as she is talking. She is expressive, tending to talk rapidly, and she is able to talk for long periods of time without getting tired. In fact, if she is forced to be quiet in a discussion, she will sometimes get distracted. She needs to be verbal in order to stay focused.

On the other hand, I, as an introvert, need time to process thoughts and ideas. I am more reflective. When introverts talk, there are always little pauses as they wait for their brains and their mouths to get back into sync with each other. An example of this difference is seen when Jan and I get ready to go to bed at night. Jan will often review the day aloud, commenting on the things we were not able to finish. I hear her thoughts and think that I need to get up and finish the things she is talking about.

I do the same thing, but I don't say anything aloud. I lie there in bed and think about my day, talking to myself about the things that needed to be done. If I were to say out loud one of the things on my list, I would need to get up and finish it (which is why I think I have to finish the things Jan is talking about).

Introverts are comfortable with silence, whereas extraverts feel as if they need to fill in the silent spaces. When an introvert and an extravert talk to each other on the phone, the conversation will often appear to be one-sided because the extravert will feel the need to fill in the introvert's silent pauses.

Introverts are comfortable with silence because they use the time to recharge their energy batteries. Solitude is restorative to the introvert, whereas interaction with friends refreshes the extravert. It's important to note that sometimes extraverts look like introverts because they are burned-out on people. They want to get away to find some quiet. But when they are given some solitude or sleep, they are ready to go again. The introvert needs much more time to be restored.

The Extravert and the Introvert Relator

Which World Do I Relate To? The Outer World or the Inner World?

EXTRAVERT	INTROVERT
1. Processes information immediately (Speaks without pauses)	Processes information slowly (Pauses when speaking)
2. Thinks out loud	Thinks before speaking
3. Feels that he or she must fill the silent spaces in conversation	Is comfortable with silence
4. Is refreshed by interacting with people	Finds solitude restorative
5. Relates to the outer world of people and things	Relates to the inner world of ideas and thoughts
6. Enjoys talking to lots of people	Prefers talking to a few people, one at a time
7. Needs confirmation from other people about who he or she is	Confirmation about who he or she is comes from an inner source
8. Likes a new challenge and is willing to jump in and try something new	Prefers to stand back and check out a new situation before committing
9. Likes to work with people close by	Enjoys working alone, without interruption
10. Is distracted by things in immediate environment	Is focused and can more easily shut out distraction

The extraverts' need to express themselves often puts them in the position of invading the introverts' private space. Jan longs for interaction, whereas I look for time alone. This usually gives the extravert a greater degree of confidence in group activity. Often the bigger the group, the greater the challenge, while, for the extravert, the small group can be threatening since it could be limiting and/or boring.

In groups, introverts, like me, will usually look for someone who shares a common interest with them and then find a quiet place to sit and talk. If they are forced into large groups, they will create their own small group of one or two others. They will feel comfortable in the large group only if they are in charge and can call the shots. That's why introverts may sometimes be comfortable speaking to large groups: They are in charge.

Extraverts, like Jan, are much more open about trying new things. They are more adventurous and appear much more skilled in dealing with the external world. They have a relaxed and confident attitude that makes them willing to jump into something new in order to understand it.

Introverts, like me, are much more reserved and cautious. They are not as comfortable with the external world, so they want to check it out first. I will stand back and observe while Jan plunges in. The higher percentage of extraverts in the United States is quite opposite to the number of extraverts in England. We like to speculate that perhaps when the pilgrims were preparing to come to America, all the extraverts were on the ship, willing to plunge into the unknown. All the introverts were on the dock saying, "You check it out first and then come back and tell us about it. Maybe then we'll get on the next boat."

To help people discover whether they are extraverts or introverts, we always ask them to think back to their childhood. "Do you think of yourself as someone who was happy playing alone most of the time?" we ask. "Were one or two good friends more than enough? If so, you are probably an introvert. If you had difficulty playing alone for very long or preferred spending time with Mom or Dad if you didn't have friends around, then you are probably an extra-vert."

In a work setting, extraverts will want other people working around them. When the job gets tedious or boring, they love to be able to talk with someone in order to get recharged. Introverts like to work alone without interruption. They would love to be able to close the door and hang a "Do Not Disturb" sign on the door when they have a project to work on.

If you have some difficulty deciding which is your more dominant trait, think about which is more diffi-cult for you. Do you have a harder time putting up with a lot of people around? Or do you struggle more with sitting still and enjoying solitude? The social pressures to be an extravert lead a lot of introverts to work hard at extraverted behaviors. But it is always work and requires effort.

Is Your Mate an Extravert or an Introvert?

You may identify with Jan, and your spouse may seem to be similar to me. We suggest that you retake the short quiz from the beginning of this chapter for your mate. Check the letter below that applies to your spouse.

1. Your spouse has been invited to a party and your spouse knows only the host and the hostess. He or she is obligated to go. Will your spouse tend to:
A. Find it stimulating to meet new and interesting people and enjoy talking to this group or that group?
B. Find someone who is interested in something your spouse is interested in and spend most of the evening sitting somewhere and talking with one person at a time?

2.The hostess has planned several games for everyone to play. Your spouse has never heard of the first game. Would he or she tend to:
A. Decide to play the game in order to understand it?

B. Want to let others play first so he or she can watch in order to understand the game?

3. On the way home your spouse realizes that it has been a pleasant evening. Would your spouse tend to:

A. Find that he or she has renewed energy and is keyed up because of the stimulating evening?

B. Find that in spite of the enjoyment of the evening, he or she is tired and feels drained?

4. Your spouse has had a very tiring day. When he or she comes home in the evening, would your spouse usually tend to:

A. Want to call a friend or two and meet for dinner?

B. Take the phone off the hook so he or she could have a quiet evening alone?

5. If something enters your spouse's mind, does he or she usually tend to:

A. Say it almost immediately?

B. Think about it before he or she talks about it?

6. If there is a long pause in a conversation, does your spouse:

A. Feel as if he or she should fill the silence by saying something?

B. Hardly notice the pause at all or find it refreshing?

7. Does your spouse enjoy working:

A. With lots of people around him or her?

B. Alone so that there is little interruption?

8. When your spouse was a child, did he or she:

A. Need to have lots of friends around?

B. Tend to be quite happy playing alone?

9. Does your spouse tend to:

A. Jump right in when faced with a new challenge?

B. Prefer to stand back and check out a new situation before committing?

How did your spouse score? More A's than B's? If so, he or she is an extravert. If your mate scored more B's than A's, then he or she is an introvert. You might even ask your spouse to take the quiz. Then compare your assessment to his or her results to see if they agree. Don't be surprised if you see your spouse differently than he or she sees himself or herself.

My spouse is an _____relator.

We've known husbands, for instance, who thought their wives were extraverts. When the wives take the test, their answers indicate that they are introverts. The husbands may be seeing the wives as they wish they were. Or the husbands may be more accurate than the wives in assessing their personalities. It works both ways. Either way, we suggest that the couple discuss the results, which often opens up some real possibilities for increased understanding of one another and opportunity for greater intimacy with each other.

How We Attract and Interact

The old adage that opposites attract certainly contains a lot of truth, especially in regard to these traits. Jan and I are opposites, as you already realize. You and your spouse may also be opposites. To the extravert, the introvert appears to be mysterious and to have it all together. The quiet reserve comes across as a quiet confidence. On the other hand, the introvert looks at the extravert and envies his or her ability to do so many things. The extravert can meet people, interact with ease, and tackle any project.

But after a while, problems arise. To the extravert, introverts appear slow and plodding, even morbid. They take too much time to deliberate before acting. Extraverts end up feeling shut out of the inner world of the introvert, bothered by the many silences. Jan often says that I don't talk with her. I tell her I am always having a two-way conversation—she talks to me, and I talk to me; I just don't talk out loud enough.

To the introvert, after a while, the extravert appears to be spread too thin, distracted and pressuring. Introverts wonder why the extraverts can't just shut things out and focus on them.

The Potential Problems in Relationships

When You Are Both Extraverts

When two extraverts are in a relationship, there is often a lot of activity. They are on the "go" a lot. There are always a lot of people around, and talk flows easily. We spent an evening recently with a couple who were very extraverted, especially the husband. From the time he entered the room, he directed the conversation. If he left the room, his wife picked up the conversation and directed it. There were several couples there, and we watched the extraverts compete for the floor.

They weren't looking for attention this way; it was much more natural than that. They just needed to express themselves verbally. To the introverts in the group, the conversation seemed superficial, yet enjoyable. When the man led the conversation, everyone talked about cars. When his wife was talking, the conversation was about clothes and houses. They loved the interaction. Nothing wrong with that—except that the introverts wanted more, even though they didn't seem willing to give it.

It is not unusual for one of the partners to be more comfortable with introversion than the other and, thus, play the role of the introvert in the marriage but be an extravert in other areas of their life.

When You Are Both Introverts

When two introverts are in a relationship together, things are much quieter. There's no competition to see who can plan something exciting all the time. Instead, each person is looking for ways to protect his or her territory. They will often plan things with friends several weeks in advance. If it's far enough ahead, it doesn't feel like pressure. But as the time approaches, the two introverts start to feel crowded and begin to look for a polite way to get out of things.

They will enjoy a small dinner party of two or three other couples at most. It will probably be the same people most of the time, but that allows them to develop a deeper friendship and talk about ideas at a deeper level. The extraverted couple may think of this lifestyle as boring, but the introverted couple doesn't feel that way. In fact, they think the extraverted couple's lifestyle is hectic and chaotic.

Most couples will show the pattern of opposites even though they may come out on the same side of the test. The reason for this is that their scores are on a linear continuum; in relation to each other, one will act more introverted, even though both are extraverts. (Or the opposite can be true—one will act more extraverted than the other, even though both are introverts.)

Husband Is an Extravert, Wife Is an Introvert

When the man is the extravert and the woman is the introvert (or that is the way they relate to each other), we don't find too many adjustment problems. Perhaps it is because this type of interaction is closer to the role stereotypes of our culture: the man is gregarious and outgoing; the woman is more reserved and doesn't push herself to the forefront.

However, in a relationship like this, the extraverted man often misunderstands the introverted woman. He may assume that her quietness is just a part of her "submissiveness." She may play that role for some time, but eventually she will feel she has been taken for granted. Maybe he hasn't shown any interest in who she really is, in her inner self. Over the years a lot of anger can build up in a woman in this position.

Husband Is an Introvert, Wife Is an Extravert

The more overt problems take place in the relationship when the man is more introverted and the woman more extraverted. Here we get into the traditional nagging-rejecting syndrome, where the woman is doing all the acting and all the talking, and the man is assumed not to care because he never says anything. The more she talks, the less he talks. The more this goes on, the more the woman feels responsible for everything and resents the man for his lack of responsibility for the relationship. She gets tired of being the one to initiate and plan everything. He, in turn, begins to feel that he's a fifth wheel whose only purpose is to pay the bills. He gets tired of her pressure and digs in his heels even further.

We've found that once couples realize that their differences are a part of their original attraction to each other, the pressure begins to let up. Each person can begin to say, "When you act that way, I don't have to take it personally as an affront or challenge to me. I don't have to be so threatened by it. It's a natural part of you."

After understanding their differences, couples have come back to tell us that the things that used to drive them crazy about each other are now rather comical, mostly because they no longer see this behavior as a personal attack. Now, they can laugh at the very thing that used to be the center of controversy. Jan can now say to herself that I'm not rejecting her, I'm just processing. And I can say to myself that she is not nagging or pressuring me, she's just thinking out loud.

An example of our differences took place early one morning as we sat in a fog-bound airport. I found a seat in the waiting area, at the end of a row, and immediately started to read a book. Jan sat next to me, and when someone sat next to her, she would strike up a conversation with the person or they would start talking to her. They seemed to know she was open to conversation. She would have a good time talking with each person, then give me the nudge with her elbow, indicating that she wanted me to meet the person. Over the two-hour delay, I met three or four "interesting" people.

When we got on the plane, I sat on the aisle, and she sat in the middle. We talked a while, and then I started reading again. (She really didn't mind my reading.) Then she started talking to the man sitting by the window. Soon I got the nudge with the elbow that indicated it was time for me to meet the man. He turned out to be a doctor from an area about eighty miles from where we lived. When I asked her later why she needed me to talk to the doctor on the plane, she replied, "You never know when you might need a doctor up in that area. And anyway, he was interesting."

If you are an extravert, you might think I was shutting Jan out, but remember, this behavior is typical of an introvert. If you are an introvert, you can probably identify with my role and feel the pressure of Jan's wanting me to meet and talk with everyone. But if you understand the differences, you might be able to laugh with us and celebrate how God has made each of us.

Remember, the key is not in changing yourself or the other person so you can be the same. The key is to accept what you are and what the other person is, seek to understand the differences, and then learn how to laugh at what you used to take so personally.

Intimate Partners Learn to Communicate Through Silence

An interesting thing has occurred in our extravert/introvert relationship. I love silence, and Jan typically gets uncomfortable with it. Jan used to have to draw me out. Over the years, as our intimacy has grown, we've found that when we are alone together I now talk at times more than Jan does. And she has become more comfortable with silence. As a result, we now use our differences to build intimacy.

Silence is a communication skill as important as speech. Our obsession with verbal communication often hides the fact that some things don't have to be said. Too much talk can clutter a relationship. Many couples find that they convey important information with a glance, a touch, or even a tone of voice.

A friend told me about the time he and his wife were sitting on a beach on the Indian Ocean at sunset. They were both so overwhelmed by the beauty of the moment that neither wanted to spoil it with words. Because they were near the equator, the day had disappeared within fifteen minutes and the night had come. But that quarter of an hour was one of their "intimate moments." As they held hands, not a word passed between them, only a slight squeezing of each other's fingers. Each had his or her own thoughts, but they had them together.

As we mentioned at the beginning of Part Two, these personality traits will build and connect to the other traits to give each of us an overall profile of who we are. At the end of each chapter, therefore, you will note your and your mate's particular traits or preferences. After you have considered all four combinations, copy these letters onto a composite profile of both your personality and your spouse's personality.

Write your preference and your spouse's in the space below:

When I relate to the world around me, I tend to be (*E*, extravert; *I*, introvert) _____.

When my spouse relates to the world, my mate tends to be (*E*, extravert; *I*, introvert) _____.

Next, we will look at another personality trait: the sensing or the intuitive observer.

4

Sensing or Intuitive Observer?

JAN AND I were driving north along the California coast one spring afternoon. Every few minutes I said to Jan, "Look at that. Isn't it beautiful!" She was busy reading something in the car, so she'd look up for a moment, say something like, "Yeah," and then turn her attention back to what she was doing.

After a while I started to get irritated with her. "Why can't you enjoy the beauty of the drive?" I asked her. "I point something out to you, and you look for a moment and then forget it. How can you really enjoy something with a quick glance? It doesn't seem that you take time to enjoy the moment."

As we talked about it, it was clear that she *could* enjoy the view and didn't need to "drink it in" in order to appreciate the beauty of what she saw. "I've always been that way," she added. "When I was in school, I could quickly review something and know it for a test. I'd go through the test, get done before most everyone else, and get excellent grades. I guess I just don't need much time to observe something." Sometimes her quickness felt more like neglect or lack of interest, especially in the early days of our marriage. At other times, I felt that she was distracted, as if anything else that might come along would capture her attention.

Once I understood that this was part of her personality style, it became easier for me to keep from personalizing it. What had been a frequent source of misunderstanding became a fascinating aspect of personality.

Sensing or Intuitive?

Here's a short quiz for you to take to see if you share traits that are similar to Jan's or are different from her style:

Are You a Sensing or Intuitive Observer?

1. When you were taking a test in school, did you usually:

A. Take the time allotted for the test, checking and double checking your answers?
B. Finish the test rather quickly, only taking the time to check for obvious errors, or maybe not even go over it?

2. When the teacher announced that a test was coming, did you feel more comfortable if the test was going to be:

A. Either a multiple choice or a fill-in-the-blank test?
B. An essay test?

3. Your boss has just given you a promotion that has two possible job choices. Would you prefer:

A. Working in the general area of production and distribution?
B. Working in an area related to research and design?

4. Someone has given you a book as a gift. As you start to read it, you find that the author has a unique style, using a lot of similes and metaphors—in other words, the author has a very odd and original way of describing things. Do you find this to be:

A. Somewhat frustrating because you like authors to say what they mean in a direct style?
B. Somewhat fascinating and enjoyable?

5. You've been asked to teach a class. Before you accept, you are concerned about the type of class it will be. Would you prefer it to be:
A. A class that focuses on factual information?
B. A class that focuses a lot on theory?

6. Do you like to go through things:
A. Step by step, beginning with *A* then going to *B* and *C?*
B. Prefer a more global style of reasoning, looking at the whole and then starting where you think best?

7. When you write a memo, do you:
A. List everything in a careful order?
B. Often add more information between the lines or up the side of the paper with an arrow to show where that thought goes?

8. When you are talking, do others find that you:
A. Tend to say precisely what you mean?
B. Tend to say less than what you mean and assume that others can fill in the gaps?

How did you score? If you scored more A's than B's, you are the sensing observer. If you scored more B's than A's, you are the intuitive observer. Remember, each of us has some of both traits. We're just looking for the more dominant aspects or the one we prefer. Remember our example of left-handed and right-handed people. Record your preference, sensing or intuitive, in the space below:

I am a/an_____observer.

Sensing people enjoy the details of what is happening at the moment. They live in the now. The sensing person gathers information in a very orderly fashion to build a case. "Give me more facts," is what they say. Facts are not boring to them. They can handle routine. The sensing person finds comfort in predictability, maybe even in going home the same way each day.

In our seminars I often say, "Sensing people are often described as practical, realistic, sensible people who have their feet on the ground—down-to-earth folks."

Jan, the intuitive person, replies, "Now can you think of any more boring words than factual, down-to-earth, and realistic?" And all the intuitive people nod in agreement.

Intuitive persons are future oriented, always living in tomorrow. Everything this person is observing today has little meaning at this moment; instead it's always thought of in reference to tomorrow. Intuitive people gather information in a very global, disconnected fashion because their case is built intuitively. They are imaginative, bored-with-routine kind of people who can appear to have their heads in the clouds; they appear to be dreamers. They become annoyed by an abundance of facts, and they are always bored by routine. Intuitive people may get tired of doing things the same way all the time, for instance. They'll want to try a different way to see if it's quicker or more interesting.

The question to consider in order to understand these two types is: "How do I take in information about the world around me?" How do I gather data? Do I take a very concrete approach to things, as the sensing person does? Or do I use my intuition in an abstract way, as the intuitive person does?

An equal number of men and women prefer either the sensing trait or the intuitive trait. But, overall, in the American culture, there are three sensing people for each intuitive person.[1] Just as with the extraverted trait, a high value is placed on the sensing function. If you are an intuitive person, you may feel you are often swimming against the current.

The Worlds of Sensing and Intuitive People

Let's look at a husband and wife who are opposites in this personality trait. Tom is a sensing person who likes to deal with the known, concrete facts; Mary is an intuitive person who loves to live in the world of ideas and imagination. To Tom, Mary, the intuitive person, appears to be restless, easily bored, even fickle at times. To Mary, Tom, the sensing person, is always bordering on being dull and bogged down in routine details. He seems so cut and dried most of the time, never able to see the forest because of his interest in each tree. But routine is comfortable and predictable, not boring, to Tom. If he has a problem to solve and there is a reliable, proven way to solve it, he uses that method without even thinking twice about it. This is his forte. His gift is to gather facts in order to solve problems. Mary loves to find new ways to solve old problems. It's the only way she can get through routine tasks. Her strength is to find new avenues with which to approach a problem.

Both personality types can be creative, but they show their creativity in different ways. Tom loves to work in his wood shop, making things with his hands. He likes the feel of the wood, and he likes to see the results of his work. Mary tends to be more creative with ideas; figuring out how to do something is more interesting to her than actually doing it. Mary is always thinking of new restaurants to go to or new places to visit on their vacations. She puts colors together and imagines how they might look in a room.

Tom and Mary are particularly aware of their differences when it comes to putting a new toy together for the kids. Tom likes to sit down and read through the directions, carefully organizing the project before he begins. Mary never bothers to look at the directions.

She looks at the pieces of the toy for a moment and may glance at the picture of the finished product. Then she quickly starts putting things together, and by the time Tom has figured out the directions, she has the toy finished. She's able to visualize the finished product and simply do it. Of course, she may have a piece left over, but if the toy works, she doesn't bother with it. Meanwhile, Tom is looking through the directions again, trying to figure out where that piece should go and why the toy works without it.

Tom's and Mary's learning styles are different. Tom likes to go through things step-by-step, on a linear path; he likes to start with point A, then move to point B, and then to point C. Mary is much more circular and global; she may start at point C, grab point F, glance at point B, and know the conclusion. She doesn't need all the in-between steps in order to reach a conclusion.

The differences in their learning styles could be compared to two people on skis standing at the top of a snow-covered mountain. Sensing people ski down the side of the mountain, noticing the beauty of the scenery, the rocks, the trees, the sky, and the interesting cloud formations. They pause at places where the beauty of the view is overwhelming. Finally, after twenty minutes or so they arrive at their destination at the bottom of the hill, only to find that their intuitive mates are standing there, waiting for them.

Intuitive people do things quickly. They start down the hill and soon find a ski jump. As they fly through the air, they land at the bottom of the hill. It took them less than a minute to get there, and they sit down and wait for their sensing spouses. When those people finally arrive, the intuitive people ask them, "What on earth took you so long?" After the sensing people relate all that they have seen on the way down the mountain, they stop and ask the intuitive people, "How did you get here?" Intuitive people can only say, "I don't know how, but I got here." Sensing people then reply, "It may take me longer, but at least I know how I got here." The sensing people see a lot of the detail as well, whereas intuitive people are so quick to jump to a conclusion they miss the details and sometimes miss out on the joy of the moment.

Tom, as the sensing person, lives for the now. He doesn't like to get too far into the future, dreaming up goals or ideas. If forced to become too future oriented, he tends to become very pessimistic and worried.

Mary, on the other hand, lives for tomorrow. To her, life is always just around the corner. She faces life expectantly and optimistically. If she is forced to live too much in the present moment, and loses sight of her dreams and goals, she can become depressed and disoriented. She needs a future in order to live joyfully.

As people try to determine whether they are sensing or intuitive, we sometimes ask them to think back to their childhood. Did you enjoy learning practical skills? Or did you like to exercise your imagination sometimes getting lost in your daydreams? How would you have responded, for instance, if your teacher had asked you to take a piece of paper and a pencil, look out the window for a minute, and then, after the minute was up, write down everything you had seen outside, without looking again to check?

The sensing child would be in her glory. She would start writing all the details of the scene outside. She would tell about the trees and how the wind was affecting the leaves. She would include a description of the plants and flowers and many other things that she noticed looking out the window. The intuitive child, however, may write only a sentence or two, saying, "It's a pretty day outside."

Next, the teacher might ask you to turn the paper over, look outside again, and imagine something is happening out there. Then, after a minute, you are to write out what you imagined. Now the intuitive child would be in his glory. If given enough time, he could fill several pages before the sensing child could even think of what to write.

The list below includes several traits of the sensing and the intuitive persons.

Sensing and Intuitive

How Do I Take in Information about the World Around Me?

SENSING PEOPLE	INTUITIVE PEOPLE
1. Gather information in a very orderly fashion	Gather information in a global disconnected fashion because the case is built intuitively
2. Live in the "now"	Live in the future
3. Love the world of facts	Enjoy the world of ideas
4. Practical, sensitive people with their feet on the ground	Creative, imaginative people who appear to have their heads in the clouds
5. Say precisely what they mean and mean what they say (speak with periods)	Always mean more than they say (speak with dashes)
6. Routine can be comfortable and predictable	Routine is boring

These two traits complement each other, just as the extravert and introvert traits do. Intuitive people need sensing people to help them see the pertinent facts related to a situation. They even need sensing people to help them notice what needs to be done now.

Sensing people need intuitive people to help them look ahead, especially because the intuitive people are so enthusiastic about the future. The intuitive people help the sensing people see that the joys of tomorrow are worth seeking, while the sensing help the intuitive see that the joys of the present moment are just as important.

Is Your Mate Sensing or Intuitive?

Now that you understand the difference between the sensing and intuitive personalities, take the quiz again to see if your mate is sensing or intuitive.

Is Your Mate a Sensing or Intuitive Observer?

1. When your mate was in school and was taking a test, did he or she usually:
A. Take the time allotted for the test, checking and double checking his or her answers?
B. Finish the test rather quickly, only taking the time to check for obvious errors, or maybe not even go over it?

2. When the teacher announced that a test was coming, would your spouse feel more comfortable if the test was going to be:
A. Either a multiple choice or a fill-in-the-blank test?
B. An essay test?

3. Your mate's boss has just given him or her a promotion that has two possible job choices. Would your spouse prefer:
A. Working in the general area of production and distribution?
B. Working in an area related to research and design?

4. Someone has given your mate a book as a gift. As he or she starts to read it, your mate finds that the author has a unique style, using a lot of similes and metaphors—in other words, the author has a very odd and original way of describing things. Would your mate find this to be:
A. Somewhat frustrating because he or she likes authors to say what they mean in a direct style?
B. Somewhat fascinating and enjoyable?

5. Your mate has been asked to teach a class. Before accepting, your mate is concerned about the type of class it will be. Would your mate prefer it to be:
A. A class that focuses on factual information?
B. A class that focuses a lot on theory?

6. Does your mate like to go through things:
A. Step by step, beginning with A then going to B and C?
B. Prefer a more global style of reasoning, looking at the whole and then starting where he or she thinks best?

7. When your mate writes a memo, does he or she:
A. List everything in a careful order?
B. Often add more information between the lines or up the side of the paper with an arrow to show where that thought goes?

8. When your mate talks to you, do you find that he or she:
A. Tends to say precisely what he or she means?
B. Tends to say less than what he or she means and always assumes that you can fill in the gaps?

How did your mate score? If your mate scored more A's than B's, he or she is a sensing person. If your mate scored more B's than A's, he or she is an intuitive person. Remember, each of us has some of each trait. We're just looking for the more dominant one.

My mate is a/an _____observer.

Again we suggest that you and your spouse compare your evaluations of each other. If your evaluations differ, you might try to determine whether one of you is evaluating the other as he or she would like a spouse to be. Or is the spouse more objective in the evaluation than he or she usually is? As we've mentioned before, this discussion can bring you and your spouse closer together if the traits are seen as equally good and valid.

When a sensing person and an intuitive person

marry, they may have some initial problems in communicating with each other.

The Battle Between the Period and the Dash

The mind of the sensing person is organized differently from the mind of the intuitive person. Neither one is better than the other; they are just different. And this difference is most noticed in the area of communication. Couples who understand this difference are able to develop intimacy more easily because poor communication is one of the primary barriers to closeness.

We've noticed that intuitive people have a difficult time finishing their sentences. Ideas run through their minds so quickly that, before they can finish a sentence, they are on to a new thought. Sometimes two intuitive people who have known each other well for a number of years can talk together, and an outsider who is listening may think that neither of them ever completes a thought. Yet, they understand each other perfectly. It's like they speak in a private code.

Sensing people are literal communicators who tend to say precisely what they mean. It's like they speak with periods at the end of complete sentences. Intuitive persons are inferential communicators who say less than what they mean and always assume that the other person can fill in the gaps. It's like they speak with dashes and incomplete sentences.

Tom and Mary are true to their traits. And they experienced a great deal of frustration and hurt in this area of their relationship. In Chapter 2 we saw that Mary felt Tom should be able to read her mind. That's because, as an intuitive, Mary assumed that those who cared for her should and could actually read between the lines.

Here's an example of how it worked for them: Whenever Tom and Mary talked about anything, Tom would talk with complete sentences and periods at the end of his sentences. Mary would talk with dashes, leaving out a lot of information that she just assumed Tom knew and understood. They were talking like a sensing person and an intuitive person would talk. But that was only the basis of the problem, not the heart of it.

The problem was compounded by the way they listened. Each listened to the other according to his or her specific trait, assuming that the other person was talking as he or she would talk. Tom assumed that Mary was a literal communicator, so he would erase Mary's dashes and put in periods. Mary assumed that Tom was an inferential communicator, so she would erase his periods and put in dashes. You can imagine the kind of problems this created.

Here's an example: Tom and Mary had a second home, which was quite large, in the mountains nearby. They often used it to entertain business associates and customers. Tom came home one Friday afternoon and said to Mary, "Let's go to the mountains." "No," Mary responded, "I don't think so." "Well," Tom said, "I've got several business people coming there, so I need to go. I'll see you Sunday." And he left.

Well, while Tom was gone, Mary started to steam. By the time Tom came home on Sunday, she was ready to explode. And he was confused. As they got into the heat of the argument, she said things like, "You should have known I wanted to go! Don't you have a brain in your head?" Tom countered with, "But

you said you didn't want to go! What's your problem?"

On and on it went with neither one understanding
that the heart of the problem was the way they listened to each other.

When Tom, the sensing person, asked Mary, the
intuitive person, if she would like to go to the mountains, he took her answer, which was "No—" and
changed it to "No." In writing, the difference is clear,
but when you're listening to someone, and your listening is based on some personal assumptions, that's
an easy mistake to make.

Part of Tom's defense included the statement, "But
you said. . . ." And part of Mary's complaint was, "I
know I might have said that, but you should know
that's not what I meant!"

As they described their most recent argument, I
asked Mary what her "No" had meant. She had had
time to think about it and was now able to identify
what she assumed Tom understood. She said, "I
meant 'No—I don't think I want to go until you tell
me who else is going to be there.' Or 'No—I can't go
right now because I'm expecting an important call
right after dinner, and then I may want to go.' Or 'No
—I really want to spend some time alone with you.
When can we plan that?' "

Tom sat there listening to what Mary was saying,
and his only response was, "Why doesn't she just say
that? Why does she just say 'No'?" I tried to explain to
him the inferential nature of the intuitive's communication style, but it didn't make sense to him.

I described the intuitive's mind as being in two
parts, a part that the intuitive person is conscious of
and a part that he or she is aware of but cannot articulate. I explained to Tom that what Mary was trying to
communicate to him was like an iceberg. About 10

percent of it is above the water, where it can be seen and articulated. But about 90 percent of it is underwater, and Mary could not articulate it until more popped to the surface in a couple of days, or until someone helped her understand what she was saying.

While I explained this to Tom, Mary sat there, nodding her head in agreement. When I finished I expected Tom to act as if some light had just gone on in his mind. But he looked at me with a blank face and asked again, "But why can't she just say it?"

Then I asked him, "When you leave Mary a note, how do you word it?"

"I write out what I want to say to her, just like I was writing her a letter."

"What do Mary's notes to you look like?" I asked.

"They're impossible to understand sometimes," he answered. "She has a couple of words and then a dash. I sometimes have to stand there and look at that note for several minutes before I can understand it."

I explained to him that he was trying to understand the part of the iceberg that was still underwater—that was what the written dash represented. Tom had to remind himself that whenever Mary said something to him, it was followed by a dash, and he needed to discover the words that would fill in that dash.

Now, it's important to know that you will never find out what the dash of the intuitive person means by asking a question. If that is what you do, you will simply get a rehash of the information that has already been given. Instead, the sensing person must paraphrase back to the intuitive person what he or she heard the intuitive person say, and then allow the intuitive person to add to what has been said already. And this paraphrasing needs to be repeated until the

intuitive person says, "Yes, that's what I've been trying to say to you."

The conversation might go something like this:

Tom: Let's go to the mountains.
Mary: No—I don't think so.
Tom: You don't want to go? *(a paraphrase of what she
has just said)*
Mary: Not exactly. I just can't go now.
Tom: You mean you might go later this evening or
tomorrow morning? *(another paraphrase)*
Mary: Yes, I'm expecting an important call right after
dinner, and then I might be able to get ready and
go.
Tom: Oh, okay.

It may seem awkward to paraphrase, but in Tom
and Mary's case, when Tom finally understood his
part, it was like finding a lost key that opened an
important door.

When intuitive people write out a first draft of a
note or memo and then look at what they wrote, they
will often add more information between the lines or
up the side of the paper with an arrow to show where
that thought goes. They do this because when they
write, they can see the part of the iceberg that is still
underwater.

The problem is not one-sided. When Mary listens to
Tom, she automatically erases the period he puts at
the end of his sentence and puts a dash in its place.
This creates a similar type of problem.

Mary wants Tom to be able to read her mind, but at
the same time she assumes that she can read his
mind. For example, Tom talked about a recent discussion in which Mary suggested they go out for dinner.
Tom told her that he really didn't want to go out, and

he felt that was the end of the subject. He said "No" with a period at the end of the sentence. Mary erased the period and put in a dash.

In her mind, she assumed that Tom's "No" was like her "No." She came back to Tom a couple of minutes later and said, "I know, you're just worried about whether we have enough money to eat out again." With some irritation, Tom said he told her that wasn't the case; he just didn't want to go out to eat.

A few minutes later, Mary suggested they try a new restaurant she had heard about recently. Tom repeated his "No." Then Mary said, "I'm sorry, I just thought you didn't want to have to decide where to go if we went out to eat." A little later, Mary again approached Tom and said, "I checked with the kids and they don't want to go out to eat, so it would be just you and me."

This time Tom responded with an explosive "No!" and jumped on her for always trying to read his mind. "My 'no' means no and nothing more! I just don't want to go out to eat! Is that so hard for you to understand?"

As Tom related that exchange, Mary sat with an all-knowing smile on her face. When he finished, she said she was sure he wanted to go out to eat that night; she just hadn't been able to figure out what the problem was. Tom jumped in and said, "The only problem is that you never take me at my word. You're always assuming that I mean something other than what I said."

Mary needed to paraphrase what she thought she heard Tom say to her so that he could trim out all of the inferences she had added and bring her back to precisely what he had said.

Their conversation might go something like this:

Mary: Let's go out for dinner tonight.

Tom: No, I don't want to go out tonight.

Mary: You mean you don't know where we should go? *(a paraphrase with Mary's interpretation added)*

Tom: No, I don't want to go out tonight.

Mary: You mean you think we've spent too much eating out this month? *(another paraphrase with her interpretation added)*

Tom: No, I just don't want to go out.

Mary: You really mean you don't want to go out?

Tom: Yes, that's right!

Couples who have practiced this paraphrasing report back that in many cases they started to really hear what the other person was trying to say. This is true for marriage relationships, for parent-child relationships, and for casual and business relationships as well.

A man attending one of our seminars scored himself as an intuitive. He related to me on a break that he was an engineer. Most engineers are sensing people, but he came from that generation in which young men going to college assumed they would be engineers, whether it fit their personalities or not.

He was now in a position where he managed a team of twelve engineers. His problem was that his team never did what he told them to do. I suggested that probably they did precisely what he told them to do. But, since he was an inferential communicator, he wasn't telling them what he thought he was telling them.

Now you can't go around the workplace paraphrasing everyone, so I suggested that he follow up each of his planning meetings with a written summary of what he wanted his team to do. And I told him to make the summary as complete as he possibly could. I then asked him to call me and let me know what happened.

Several weeks later he called and said that my suggestion was working beautifully. At first, several of his engineering team would come back to him and say, "I didn't know you meant for me to do all of this." His written summary was filling in the blanks, it was bringing the whole iceberg to the surface, and everyone was a lot happier.

Tom and Mary may need to write notes to each other if the paraphrasing feels too contrived. But they need to reflect on what they are writing—especially Mary so she can make sure her notes say what she means. And Mary needs to work at not reading into Tom's letter things that are not there. It's equally difficult for both the sensing person and the intuitive person to adjust to the other style of communication.

These traits are on a continuum so that both husband and wife can be on the same side of the scale but see the spouse as if he or she were on the opposite side. For example, you may have answered most of the questions at the beginning of the chapter as a sensing person, seven A's and one B. Your spouse may have scored five A's and three B's. You are both sensing people, but in your relation to each other you will be seen as the sensing person and your spouse will be seen as the intuitive person. Since the interpretation of the scale is relative to the other person in the relationship, many of us will experience each other as opposites. Jan and I are both intuitive, but, as you saw in the beginning of the chapter, I am more comfortable with the sensing trait than Jan is, so we sometimes seem to be opposites. It's important that we understand the differences between us and find ways to bridge the gap so we can work on building close-ness.

Take a moment now to note your tendency and your mate's tendency in the spaces below:

When I take in information about the world around me, I tend to be (*S*, sensing; *N*, intuitive)_____.

When my mate takes in information about the world, my mate's preference is (*S*, sensing; *N*, intuitive)_____.

Now let's look at the third group of personality traits: thinking or feeling.

5

Thinking or Feeling Decision Maker?

I'VE ALREADY MENTIONED my tendency to personalize things. I even take things personally that have nothing to do with me. You can imagine how this affected my relationship with Jan over the years. If Jan was upset about anything at all, I was convinced she was upset with me. I would ask repeatedly what she was upset about, and then she would get upset with me for my incessant nagging and ridiculous assertion that I must have done something to upset her. (I'm talking about the times I really hadn't done anything to upset her!)

This didn't do much for our relationship. If every time Jan didn't quite feel up to what I thought was par, I would respond with a barrage of questions: "What's wrong? What have I done to upset you?"

Does this sound familiar? Take this short quiz to help you see if you are a feeling person, as I am, or a thinking person.

Are You a Thinking or Feeling Decision Maker?

1. You are involved in a discussion with several friends. As the discussion continues, it gets rather heated; people have differ-

ing opinions, and they feel quite strongly about their positions. As the discussion ends, you are concerned that:

A. There be a consistent summary of what has been discussed.
B. People are still happy with each other and that the discussion did not hurt any friendships.

2. A friend of yours is quite concerned about a particularly difficult situation that needs to be discussed and resolved. After you have talked together, you ask your friend why he or she came to talk to you. The friend is likely to say:

A. "I felt confident in talking with you because you always seem to be so objective and fair about things."
B. "I felt comfortable talking with you because I knew you would understand what I was feeling."

3. You are about to purchase a new car. As you have been thinking about which car to buy, you find yourself:

A. Talking to people about what they like about their cars, and you read the consumer reports to evaluate the cars you are considering.
B. Looking at other cars as you drive and wondering which one would best suit you, considering how they look, what colors they come in, and which one is more reflective of your personality.

4. When you go to the showroom to buy the car, you will probably:

A. Know exactly what you want and what options you want, and the salesperson will not be able to sway you in your thinking about your choice.
B. Have a general idea of what you want and then look at what is available and perhaps even purchase something that was not on your list, but was "your" car.

5. When people ask you:

A. "What do you feel about . . . ?" do you usually answer, "Well, I think. . . ."?
B. "What do you think about . . . ?" do you usually answer, "Well, I feel. . . ."?

6. If your spouse is upset about something, you tend to:

A. Know that he or she may be responding to something that happened with the kids or at work.
B. Think that you are the one he or she is upset with.

7. If you had to fire a person at work, you would:

A. Know exactly why and be able to show that person what he or she had done wrong.

B. Worry and stew about it.

8. When you are solving a problem, you usually look for:

A. The formula or set of rules that will make everything fit together.

B. A solution that will make everyone happy.

How did you score on this one? If you answered with more *A*'s than *B*'s, you are a thinking decision maker. If you answered with more *B*'s than *A*'s, you are a feeling decision maker.

I am a _____ decision maker.

Thinking people can stand back and look at the situation. They make a decision from an objective viewpoint, interpreting the situation from the outside. They believe that if they gather enough data they can arrive at the truth. They are always searching for this truth, which they believe exists as an absolute. These people see things as black and white, as absolutes. If the answer seems to lie in the gray area, thinking people believe that they just haven't gathered enough data. If they can just look further, they will discover the truth.

On the other hand, feeling people always make decisions from a personal standpoint by putting themselves into the situation. They are subjective, believing that two truths can exist side by side.

The difference between a thinking person and a feeling person can be seen in the way the two make decisions, such as buying a car. Thinking people get the consumer reports and do research into different types of cars. They ask themselves, "Which is the best financial value? Which is safest?" They'll decide which criteria is most important to them and then make a decision based on that criteria. When they go to the car dealership, they'll know exactly what they want, and even that persuasive car salesman can't talk them into buying another car.

Feeling people start looking at all the cars on the road. "Which car would I like to be driving right now?" they ask themselves. "What color looks good? What make? What style?" When feeling people arrive at the car dealership, they may think, "I want a blue Honda coupe." But after they've looked around a while, they may fall in love with a metallic green Honda Accord. And that's the car they'll purchase— even if it costs more money.

The important questions to ask yourself are: How do I make a decision? Do I listen more to my head when I make good decisions, or do I listen more to my heart?

About two-thirds of men are on the thinking side and two-thirds of women are on the feeling side, even though there is an equal distribution of both preferences in the American culture.[1]

Many of our sexual stereotypes come from seeing men as analytical (thinking types) and women as emotional (feeling types). When people talk about the differences between men and women, they often refer to these stereotypes. The truth is that personality type, not sex, makes you tough-minded or tender-hearted. Feeling men are greatly relieved when they find out that almost a third of all men are just like them. The same is true of thinking women. It is neither a good thing nor a bad thing that a man is on the feeling side or that a woman is on the thinking side. It just is. The key is what we do with our preference.

The Worlds of Thinking and Feeling

The thinking person uses pro-and-con lists of facts in order to arrive at the best decision. The feeling person will probably make a bad decision if he or she relies only on factual information. The feeling person needs to look at the values and the emotions involved in order to make a good decision.

The way we handle our emotions is related to our preference on this trait, even though the trait has nothing directly to do with emotions. Those who score on the thinking side are often uncomfortable talking about the area of feelings. They may also not be as comfortable in the area of aesthetics and the cultivation of relationships. To others, they appear cool and aloof; sometimes they are accused of having ice in their veins, even though they are very sensitive.

Feeling persons, on the other hand, can be quite comfortable in the area of emotions. They are usually aware of what they are feeling and can tune in to what others around them are feeling as well. When they make a decision, they are concerned about how it will affect the others involved.

It is interesting to compare how these two types of people react on a jury. Thinking people are primarily concerned with justice and fairness. They want to look at the objective facts, find the truth, and then make a decision in line with this data. They tend to see things in black and white, assuming that someone is always either right or wrong; there is no gray in-between. If it is not clear what the verdict should be, it is simply a matter of not having all the facts.

The feeling person on a jury will be primarily concerned with mercy. He or she will want to look beyond the facts to the circumstances that are involved. Why did the person do what he or she did? If there are mitigating circumstances, feeling persons will tend to be sympathetic and want to give the accused the benefit of the doubt. This often puts them in a bind because they can see both sides of an issue. The thinking person will watch this vascillation and consider the feeling person to be "wishy-washy."

Thinking or Feeling Decision Maker

How Do I Make a Decision?

THINKING DECISION MAKER	FEELING DECISION MAKER
1. Stand back and make a decision from an outside, objective viewpoint	Make decisions from a personal, subjective viewpoint
2. Believe that if you gather enough information you can arrive at the truth	Believe more in values and in considering the people involved
3. See truth as an absolute	See gray areas that complicate the truth
4. Make decisions from a list of pro-and-con facts	Make decisions from emotions, sentiment, and values
5. Uncomfortable talking about feelings	Comfortable expressing feelings
6. Look for the formula or set of rules that makes everything fit	Look for a solution that will make everyone happy

Feeling people often care too much about all sides of an issue. If they have to fire a person at work, they will worry and stew over it all night long, thinking of every side of the problem. By the time they actually fire the person, they have skirted around the issue so much that the person being fired is confused and upset and ends up resenting them.

When the thinking person is required to fire someone, the task is quite simple. Although he is often unaware of the feelings of others, he does strive for a sense of fairness in his decisions. The person being fired knows exactly where he or she stands and may even say "Thank you" as the discussion ends, because it feels as if justice has been served.

Another way to understand the inner world of these two types of people is to look at where they seek harmony. Thinking decision makers are always seeking harmony in the objective world of facts and information. They want everything to fit into its proper place. So they look for the formula, or set of rules, that will make everything fit together.

Feeling decision makers are looking for harmony in the area of emotions and relationships. They need everyone to be happy and will expend massive amounts of energy to see that people are properly "in place" in relation to one another. They will overextend themselves in serving others so that everyone can be happy.

In organizing their worlds, thinking people will want everything to be efficient, and they focus on what is true or factual. Feeling people will be more concerned with the aesthetics. They value appearance more than efficiency. It's not that they don't appreciate the opposite value; it is a matter of priority. The feeling person's priority is people, so the feeling person wants to create a pleasant environment for people to enjoy.

If you have difficulty in being clear about which type you are, it often helps to look at which trait you need to work the hardest at. Do you have a difficult time reading other people's feelings, being tactful, saying the right thing at the right time, or really empathizing with someone else's pain? If so, you are probably a thinking person. Or do you have to work hard at analyzing things logically, staying objective, and not personalizing things? If so, you are probably a feeling person.

Is Your Mate a Thinking or a Feeling Person?

Now that you understand the two personality traits, take the same quiz for your mate.

Is Your Mate a Thinking or Feeling Decision Maker?

1. Your mate is involved in a discussion with several friends. As the discussion continues, it gets rather heated; people have differing opinions, and they feel quite strongly about their positions. As the discussion ends, your mate is concerned that:
A. There be a consistent summary of what has been discussed.
B. People are still happy with each other and that the discussion did not hurt any friendships.

2. A friend of your mate's is quite concerned about a particularly difficult situation that needs to be discussed and resolved. After they have talked together, your mate asks the friend why he or she came to talk. The friend is more likely to say:
A. "I felt confident in talking with you because you always seem to be so objective and fair about things."
B. "I felt comfortable talking with you because I knew you would understand what I was feeling."

3. Your mate is about to purchase a new car. As your mate has been thinking about which car to buy, he or she would:
A. Talk to people about what they like about their cars and read the consumer reports to evaluate the cars he or she is considering.
B. Look at other cars as he or she drives and wonder which one would best suit him or her, considering how they look, what colors they come in, and which one is more reflective of your spouse's personality.

4. When your mate goes to the showroom to buy the car, he or she will probably:
A. Know exactly what he or she wants, and the salesperson will not be able to sway your spouse.

B. Have a general idea of what he or she wants and then look at what is available and perhaps even purchase something that was not on his or her list.

5. When people ask your mate:

A. "What do you feel about . . . ?" he or she usually answers, "Well, I think. . . ."

B. "What do you think about . . . ?" he or she usually answers, "Well, I feel. . . ."

6. If you are upset about something, your spouse tends to:

A. Know that you have probably had a bad day at work or with the kids.

B. Think that you are upset with him or her.

7. If your spouse had to fire a person at work, he or she would:

A. Know exactly why and be able to show that person what he or she had done wrong.

B. Worry and stew about it.

8. When your spouse is solving a problem, he or she would usually look for:

A. The formula or set of rules that will make everything fit together.

B. A solution that will make everyone happy.

How did your mate score on this one? If he or she had more *A*'s than *B*'s, your spouse is a thinking decision maker. If he or she had more *B*'s than *A*'s, your spouse is a feeling decision maker.

My mate is a _____ decision maker.

Again it would be helpful to have your spouse also take the test to evaluate his or her own personality traits and yours. Then compare your answers as you have before.

How Thinking and Feeling People Are Attracted to Each Other

Again, opposites often attract each other. The thinking person will find that the feeling person fills in the blind spots in the thinking person's personality. If the two learn how to make these traits complement each other, rather than antagonize each other, it really can be nice. But before that happens some predictable pitfalls block our way to intimacy.

Usually thinking people intimidate feeling people because thinking persons can give reasons for their decisions. Feeling people know what they believe to be right, but they cannot always give specific reasons. "I just know it inside" is what they will usually say.

I remember talking with Jay, who was a thinking person and felt everyone else should be also. He told me that in his family whenever anyone wanted anything, they had to give him three good reasons or he would not even consider the request. One of his sons was also a thinking decision maker and was just as objective as his father, so he could always come up with three good reasons why he should stay out later or have a new stereo. The other son always lost out, not because his dad didn't love him as much—which was what he thought—but because this son was a feeling person who could say only, "I just know I need it."

This "three-good-reason rule" applied to Jay's wife as well as to his kids. She was also a feeling person. She saw her husband's seeming disregard for her wants as a lack of love, and she was very, very angry about this until she understood her husband's personality type. Then she began to see that his actions were not directed *against* anyone. They were a normal part of his personality.

The feeling person is often looking for someone who is able to make an objective decision, a task right up the thinking person's alley. On the other hand, the thinking person is looking for someone who is compassionate and able to express his or her emotions. Of course, once married, they each set out to change the other one.

Megan and Steve fit the stereotypical couple in terms of these two traits. Megan is a feeling person, Steve a thinking one. Megan wants harmony in their relationship and will do just about anything to foster peace. Steve sees things as black and white, none of this undefinable emotion is allowed, at least not too much.

Being a thinking person, Steve likes to have the data lined up. He may even count on his fingers as he runs through the points as to why Megan shouldn't worry about their marriage.

Steve would say, "First, I am the breadwinner, and I am doing a good job in that area of our lives. I work a lot because that is a measure of how much I care about you and our family. Second, I think that you spend too much time brooding over our relationship."

"If it's working, don't mess with it" is Steve's motto. And to him, their marriage is working as evidenced by their income, their house, their cars, and the other things that he provides as the breadwinner.

"Third," Steve would continue, "I'm at the stage of my career where I cannot let up, and you need to understand that. We discussed this before we got married, and you need to remember that the deal hasn't really changed since then. Fourth, if you would just get your emotional stuff under control, you would see what a good deal you have."

Steve could have probably added a number of

other points in his attempt to logically convince Megan that she should relax and not make waves, but by the third point he had lost her. She wasn't interested in what was true or whether she liked it or not; she just wanted things to be good and to feel good as well. As they argued about these things it was like they were speaking different languages. They could repeat the words the other person said, but neither of them could hear what was really being said.

Feeling wives, like Megan, insist that their thinking husbands show their feelings more. After several years of attempting to change Steve, Megan complained that she hardly knew her husband, since he never opened up about his feelings. Wives sometimes push husbands like Steve to tell them what they are feeling. The husband's response usually begins, "Well, I think. . . ." She'll stop him and say, "I don't want to know what you are thinking, I want to know what you are feeling!" She'll stress this several times, and they usually will end up silent and more frustrated, not because he did not have any feelings, but because he did not know how to express them. Yet if she would suggest feeling words to him, like "Are you angry or sad or disappointed?" he would say, "Yes, that's how I feel. I'm angry about that."

When pushed to describe his feelings, the thinking husband, like Steve, is probably sitting there saying either to himself or to his wife, "Why can't you just be logical for once? Use your head!" When he says this to her, she probably shows a lot of emotion, either losing her temper, breaking into tears, or both—neither of which appears to be very logical to the thinking husband.

Yet, these two traits do not need to be oppositional. If Megan can let go of some of her responsibility for the emotional temperature of the marriage, she may get Steve's attention. Once she does that, she can be available to help Steve understand the importance of his emotional input. Each person needs to understand his or her own strengths and weaknesses in relation to these two traits and begin to develop some comfort in the opposite area.

When the roles are reversed, with the wife being a thinking person and the husband a feeling person, the problem doesn't seem to be so severe. Although the woman may predominantly be a thinking decision maker, she still has the ability to be comfortable with her feelings, perhaps because she was encouraged to express those as a child. She has been allowed to talk about her feelings and to express her personal view of things, since we stereotypically assign that role to women. She's been allowed to hurt and cry, so she learns to balance her natural bent toward thinking with her emotional side. She may grow up thinking that many of her interests are not really that feminine, but she finds other ways to express her femininity.

The man who is a feeling person, however, often develops thinking skills because he feels he's expected to be factual, tough, and blunt. He feels that he is too sensitive or not masculine enough—the opposite of our stereotypical roles—so he hides this inclination. He is never really given the opportunity to develop his strength—the feeling side of himself. Yet as he tries to cover up this side of his personality because it doesn't feel "manly," he often sets in motion an inner conflict that will interfere in his ability to relate to others. It is important for us to know our strength and to be at home in the skills of that strength so we can relate comfortably with others.

Sam and Bonnie were the opposite of the stereotypical couple, Steve and Megan. In their marriage, Sam was the feeling decision maker, and Bonnie was the thinking one. Sam had been a professional basketball player, and as we talked about his being a feeling person, he was able to show how the ability to make subjective decisions had helped him to be a better player. Sometimes, when a play would get broken up by the other team, he would have a "feeling" of what a teammate was going to do, and he would be right where he should be to make the play happen. It worked equally as well on defense as on offense.

It's important to note here that what Sam described as a "gut feeling" was different from what we discussed in an earlier chapter under the heading of intuition because we are now talking about a decision-making trait. It is also different from what we call "woman's intuition." Sam was describing a decision-making process that helped him to decide to do one thing as opposed to something else.

Bonnie agreed that he was one of the top players— a manly feat—but her problem was that Sam couldn't make decisions "like a man" in the rest of his life— when they entertained friends, for instance. After a home game they would get a bunch of friends together for dinner. Bonnie felt Sam should decide which restaurant to go to. Sam would try to evaluate objectively, as a thinking person would, who was there and where they would all like to eat. He would mention the place as he joined the group after the game. As soon as he did so, he could tell by Bonnie's face that he had made the worst possible decision.

We met with both of them one day for counseling and suggested a solution. "Sam, why not try deciding where to go to eat the same way you decide whether or not to go right or left on the court when the play starts? Then see what happens." (We were telling him to use his feeling trait when making a decision rather than trying to use the objective process a thinking person would use.)

They wrote to us a couple of months later. "It's working perfectly," they said. "So well, in fact, that we've also applied it to our financial decisions." They'd always had a couple of financial professionals advise them about their investments, which was Bonnie's thinking way of making a decision. The last time they'd met with the professionals, however, Sam had questioned their advice. "They think we should do this," he said, "but something about it just doesn't feel right to me." And he'd been right. It turned out to be a poor investment.

"I see now I should have listened to Sam, because that's his gift," Bonnie admitted in the letter. "He couldn't tell me why, but he didn't feel that the investment was a good one." She'd learned to respect his feeling style of decision making. In fact, they were able to see that if they respected each other's decision-making style, they had all the bases covered. Bonnie, the thinking person, was skilled at looking at the objective criteria, while Sam, the feeling person, was able to pick up on the intangibles that slipped through the data, but were just as crucial to a good decision.

The key to their working together was twofold. First, Bonnie had to understand that Sam's way of making decisions was a part of his personality and that it was a strength. Second, Sam had to believe that even when he didn't have identifiable, logical reasons for his decisions, he still needed to stand by them.

Bonnie, as a thinking person, tended to be too impersonal. To her, it was obvious that she loved Sam, so why did he need to hear her say it so often? Sam, as the feeling person, wanted nourishment for his emotions. Bonnie found that it didn't take a whole lot to satisfy him; she just needed to respond to some of the things Sam told her he liked her to say or do.

It is important to stress here that one does not change these traits in order to get along. Indeed, they cannot be changed. They are part of our makeup. If we try to work directly on being the opposite, we will create inner conflicts within us that become barriers to knowing ourselves and to relating to others. Instead, if we can accept who we are and accept who the other person is, we can then develop some skills in the opposite area. These skills will always be an effort for us, but they will fill in some gaps.

Feeling people need help in looking at the objective data just as thinking people need help in looking at the emotions of the people involved. When we accept what we are and what the other person is, we can both make better decisions.

Isabel Briggs Myers, who developed the Myers-Briggs test with her mother, Katherine Briggs, said, "Understanding, appreciation, and respect make a lifelong marriage possible and good. Similarity of type is not important, except as it leads to these three . . . with them, a man and a woman will become increasingly valuable to each other and know they are contributing to each other's lives."[2]

A tendency of all feeling people is to attempt to explain the behavior of others. They want to be "fair" about things, but the feeling person's sense of fairness is related to emotions, not to actions. So they will often find themselves "defending the enemy," so to speak, in their effort to try to get the thinking person to see all sides of the issue.

The thinking person's weakness in relationships is in his or her tendency to come across as critical. Among the targets of that "natural" style of criticism will be friends, relatives, coworkers, and church members. Sometimes they actually criticize others, just as a form of amusement. If the spouse stands up for himself or herself with a mild comment, the thinking person will often get the message. In fact, gentle teasing may be the kindest way for partners to acknowledge their differences on any of these traits.

Take a moment now to note your and your spouse's tendencies in the spaces below:

When I am making decisions, I tend to be (*T,* thinking; *F,* feeling)_____.

When my spouse makes decisions, he or she tends to be (*T,* thinking; *F,* feeling)_____.

Finally, let's consider the last of the personality combinations: the judging or perceiving organizer.

6

Judging or Perceiving Organizer?

PERHAPS ONE OF the things that has allowed Jan and me to work out our differences over the years is that we are both open-ended people. We are not obsessed with tying up all the loose ends. Yet, one of our problems has been that it is easy for me to be critical of Jan, because she does not finish things or is overwhelmed by details. Of course, I am simply projecting my own weaknesses onto her and then being critical of her because she does exactly what I would have done.

This pair of traits has a lot to do with our method of organizing things. Even though both of us like our casual approach, we each wish the other would be more methodical. If we're not careful, we can get angry with each other for not doing something neither of us wants to do.

Our Christmas is an example. The wrapping papers and empty boxes sit around the floor of the family room until after lunchtime. We each expect the other to clean up, until finally the mess gets to both of us and we agree to get the garbage bag and straighten up. We have friends who are just the opposite. One Christmas we happened to stop by their house early, and we were amazed to find every scrap of wrapping paper gone and every present put away. The carpet had even been swept!

Which are you more like? Here's the last of the short quizzes to help you decide.

Are You a Judging or Perceiving Organizer?

1. Your boss gives you an important assignment that is due in two weeks. As you begin working on the project, you will:

A. Take the time to list all the separate things that will need to be done, put them in the order in which you will do them, and then begin.

B. Just begin, knowing that you will find out what you need as you go along.

2. Do you:

A. Begin to work on the project immediately so you can pace your work and have the project finished on or before the deadline?

B. Tend to wait until the deadline is close, then put on a burst of speed to finish?

3. As you work on this project, will your strength be more your ability to:

A. Follow your carefully worked-out plan?

B. Deal with the unexpected things that come up and be able to see quickly the adjustments you need to make?

4. As you work on a project, you:

A. Feel you can't relax until the job is done.

B. Stop work every so often just to relax.

5. A friend of yours calls and asks if you can drop what you are doing and meet him or her for a "fun afternoon." It is important that you finish this project, but you cannot possibly finish and meet your friend. Yet you say, "Yes, I'll meet you." As you leave your house, you:

A. Find it is very uncomfortable to leave something unfinished, and just know that having the work undone will spoil your afternoon of fun.

B. Feel excited about what you are going to do, and find that you don't even think about the unfinished work left behind until you come home that evening.

6. You enjoy working with your hands and have different crafts that you work on. Over time, you have noticed that the real joy comes:
A. In displaying and admiring the finished product.
B. In the process of working on it more than in seeing the finished product. (Sometimes this leaves you with several unfinished projects.)

7. A friend has called and arranged for a special activity two weeks in advance. As you put it on your calendar, you notice that it:
A. Feels good to have something planned for that day.
B. Feels a little unpleasant, kind of like being tied down.

8. Some people think you tend to be:
A. Predictable and inflexible.
B. Spontaneous and flexible.

9. Do you:
A. Have things organized in folders?
B. Have stacks of paper lying all over the floor in your office?

How did you score? If you had more *A*'s than *B*'s, you are a judging organizer. You are often concerned with closure. This may sound derogatory, but it simply means you are comfortable making judgments, or decisions, about things. If you scored more *B*'s than *A*'s, then you are a perceiving organizer. That means you are more comfortable taking in information than in making judgments about that information.

I am a _____ organizer.

The judging person is a public organizer. If this person's spouse wants to see a doctor bill, the judging person will say, "There's a file in the left drawer of my desk; the bill will be there, filed under D for doctor." This person can appear at times to be obsessive or compulsive about his need for order. Judging organizers are often guided by the mistaken notion that mastery of their physical and material environments is the only true source of personal satisfaction. A friend of ours has a garage that is so clean and organized it looks like a room in a well-kept home. The walls have an unusual decoration: the outlines of tools of many kinds. If you remove any of the implements hanging in the garage, the outline of that particular tool is there on the wall. Anyone would know where to put a hatchet in that garage since it's organized by the "fill-in-the-space-with-the-matching-object" system. The owner even has pictures of their garage, hanging on another wall! Judging people are always organized, whereas perceiving people are always organizing, always trying to reorganize themselves.

The perceiving person is a private organizer. If a perceiving person's spouse wants that doctor bill, the perceiving person will have to get it himself or herself. This person would pull open that left drawer of the desk, reach down to the middle of the first stack of papers, and hand the spouse the doctor bill. Perceiving people may know where their things are, but no one else can go through their stuff to find anything (and if they tried, it would be impossible since there is little obvious organization). They don't want anyone to touch their things because if anyone moves something it becomes lost. The perceiving person would then have to go through everything and reorganize all the piles.

Jan is a perceiving organizer. A few years ago she purchased large white cardboard "banker" boxes to store our things. She dutifully packed them and placed them in the garage, but she's forgotten what's in some of them—because a lot of them are labeled "To be sorted." What's inside, nobody knows.

The question you need to ask yourself to determine whether you are a judging or a perceiving organizer is "How do I organize my world?" You might also ask your spouse to answer that same question about you. Often this trait is more obvious to someone who lives with you.

If you organize and then maintain that organization, you are a judging organizer. If you organize and then allow that organization to deteriorate, you are a perceiving organizer.

In the American culture, a few more people are judging organizers than perceiving organizers, about 55 percent judging to 45 percent perceiving.[1] Judging organizers are clearly more valued in our culture and are rewarded by our corporate work system. Those who are perceiving find that the most comfortable place for them in the work force is one that gives them some autonomy, such as in sales, consulting, or store ownership.

An interesting thing occurs whenever we discuss this in a seminar. Many people score very high on the judging side, but they find that their score is more a reflection of their parental training or the demands of their jobs than their natural tendencies. As you read this chapter, or discuss it with someone who really knows you, you may decide that your comfort zone is different from what you scored.

The Inner Worlds of the Judging and Perceiving Organizer

Judging people like things organized and put away. As a result, they have the belief that everything in life should be the result of a decision; life shouldn't just happen. They feel a sense of urgency inside if they are faced with a decision, and they will move quickly to the point of deciding. Only then can they relax. They are even comfortable with the old maxim that a bad decision is better than no decision at all.

Perceiving people are the opposite. They do not understand why a decision must be forced in a situation. "Let's wait and see," they might say, hoping for more information that will help them make a better decision. When they are finally forced to decide, they feel an internal uneasiness and question whether they have made the right decision.

Each type of person treats deadlines with a different attitude. When given an assignment or task to do, the judging person will begin to work on it right away and pace his or her work in order to be finished on or before the deadline. Perceiving people usually have so many irons in the fire that the deadline ends up being an emergency alarm. Only then do they get focused on finishing the particular task. They put on a burst of speed and usually finish the project not too long after the deadline, but seldom before.

As a result of these attitudes, the judging person will appear to be driven, rigid, and inflexible, while the perceiving person appears to be indecisive and restless, an incurable procrastinator. These descriptions are only partially true, however. While perceiving people may appear indecisive, they do not have an exclusive claim to procrastination—they just appear that way. Inside, they may be just as driven to finish something as the judging person is; they are just juggling ten other things that need finishing as well— and the critical project gets priority attention.

Nor is it accurate to say that judging people are rigid, since this trait is often an extension of their work ethic. Judging people like to start something, finish it without any interruptions, and clean up the mess before they begin something else. They are a mother's delight, even if their mother isn't the same on this trait.

These traits are also obvious in the way we talk

about things. Judging people express conclusions as they talk, whether they are sharing an opinion, a plan, or a schedule. Perceiving people talk without conclusions, leaving their thoughts and ideas open-ended. They are sharing their perceptions.

Another way to understand these two styles is to look at how these persons use lists. Judging people love to make lists of the things they need to do. This is their way of organizing their lives, and part of their joy comes from crossing off something as they finish it. Some judging people will go all the way across the house to cross off their list something they have finished, simply for the joy of crossing the item off their list.

Perceiving people use lists to help them remember things or to get things out of their minds. Once they have made their lists, they may never look at them again; they may even forget where their lists are. Crossing something off their lists seems to be redundant. It was enough simply to finish the task.

The Judging or Perceiving Organizer

How Do I Organize?

JUDGING ORGANIZERS (Work Ethic)	PERCEIVING ORGANIZERS (Play Ethic)
1. Neatly organize things	Organize for a short time
2. Always organized	Always reorganizing
3. Make decisions quickly (needs closure)	Tend to put off decisions (needs open-endedness)
4. May appear driven, rigid, and inflexible	May appear indecisive, restless, and procrastinating
5. Love to make lists and get pleasure in crossing off activities as they get done	Make lists as a way to get things off their minds

6. Cannot relax until job is done	Can suspend a project if something more fun comes along
7. Do one thing at a time	Can juggle many tasks
8. Work steadily toward a deadline	Use a deadline as a time to begin
9. Get a lot done over a long period of time	Get a lot done in a short period of time

Judging people operate on the basis of a work ethic. They cannot relax until the job is finished. Perceiving people have a play ethic. They can stop anything they are doing if a better option comes along. In fact, they love their options; that's the real joy in their life.

Now that you understand the judging and perceiving personality traits, take the following quiz for your mate.

Is Your Mate a Judging or Perceiving Organizer?

1. Your mate's boss has given him or her an important assignment that is due in two weeks. As he or she begins working on the project, your spouse will:
A. Take the time to list all the separate things that will need to be done, put them in the order in which he or she will do them, and then begin.
B. Just begin, knowing that he or she will find out what he or she needs along the way to completion.

2. Does your mate:
A. Begin to work on the project immediately so he or she can pace his or her work and have the project finished on or before the deadline?
B. Tend to wait until the deadline is close, then put on a burst of speed to finish?

3. As your mate is working on that project, his or her strength will be more the ability to:
A. Follow a carefully worked-out plan.

B. Deal with the unexpected things that come up and be able to see quickly the adjustments that need to be made.

4. As your mate is working on that project he or she:
A. Feels he or she can't relax until the job is done.
B. Stops work every so often just to relax.

5. A friend of your mate has called and asked your mate to drop what he or she is doing and meet for a "fun afternoon." It is important that your mate finish the project, but your mate cannot possibly finish and meet the friend. But still he or she says, "Yes, I'll meet you." As your mate leaves the house, he or she:
A. Finds it is very uncomfortable to leave something unfinished, and just knows that having the work undone will spoil the afternoon of fun.
B. Feels excited about what he or she is going to do, and finds that he or she doesn't even think about the unfinished work until later that evening.

6. Your spouse enjoys working with his or her hands and has different crafts to work on. Over time, he or she notices that the real joy comes:
A. In displaying and admiring the finished product.
B. In the process of working on it more than in seeing the finished product. (Sometimes this leaves your mate with several unfinished projects.)

7. A friend of your mate's has called and arranged for a special activity two weeks in advance. As your spouse puts it on the calendar, he or she notices that it:
A. Feels good to have something planned for that day.
B. Feels a little unpleasant, kind of like being tied down.

8. Some people think your mate is:
A. Predictable and inflexible.
B. Spontaneous and flexible.

9. Does your mate:
A. Tend to have things organized in files?
B. Have stacks of paper lying all over the floor in his or her office?

How did your mate score? If your mate had more *A*'s than *B*'s, he or she is a judging organizer. If your mate scored more *B*'s than *A*'s, then he or she is a perceiving organizer. As we mentioned before, this trait is often more obvious to others than to ourselves, so we really encourage you to ask your mate to take both tests so you can compare the answers. Both of you will probably find some surprises in the answers.

My mate is a _____ organizer.

How They Are Attracted to Each Other

Again, you can see how judging and perceiving organizers complement each other's styles. Judging people are sometimes tired of living in their structured, organized world and would love to break free. As they watch the play ethic of the perceiving person, they long for that fun-loving approach to life. During the early stages of a relationship, they will often act a lot like the perceiving person, in that they will drop what they are doing and have some fun.

On the other hand, perceiving people get frustrated with always organizing and never actually being organized. They sometimes long for some structure in their lives or for someone who will be decisive and know where to put things. During the early stages of the relationship, they may even feel a spurt of organizational skill that puts some structure in their lives.

Judging people want some freedom from structure, but "not that much freedom." They begin to feel as if their lives are unraveling and they are losing control if things get too flexible, so they quickly go back to their strength and "tighten down the loose ends."

Perceiving people may look to their spouse to help them get organized, but will begin to feel crowded by the seemingly endless structures and start to loosen things up a bit.

How the Problems Develop

Of course, after we are in a committed relationship, we start to try to change the other person. As the focus begins to shift, judging people begin to look at perceiving people and think they are lazy and unorganized. Their play ethic feels like a character flaw, not a personality style. Instead of seeing them as playful, judging people begin to think of them as flaky and irresponsible. Perceiving people, who at first love the orderliness of judging people, become convinced they married someone who has an obsessive-compulsive disorder and may even suggest that the judging person get professional help.

One judging husband, who later admitted that what attracted him to his perceiving wife was her playful spirit, wanted to help her get organized. One weekend, when she was away visiting her family, he decided to make it easier for her to organize her kitchen. He emptied all the cupboards and the pantry, cleaned it all meticulously, and then put in new, white shelf-paper. As he put everything back into the cupboards, he took a black marker and made the shape of the item on the shelf-paper. Inside one circle, he wrote *peanut butter*. In a rectangle, he wrote *cereal*. He finished, of course, before she got home and couldn't wait for her appreciative response. After all, he was helping her get organized.

Little did he imagine the intensity of her reaction. She was livid! She took it as the ultimate insult. And for her it was, for he was saying that her personality style was inadequate, that she needed help. It didn't take very long for her to put the peanut butter where he had written *cereal* and the dishes over the word *glasses*.

Unfortunately this husband had lost sight of his appreciation of his wife's personality. When pressed, he could identify how much he enjoyed her spontaneity, her ability to manage a large number of things at one time, and her fun-loving spirit. Perhaps if he had shown her how much he appreciated these attributes, she might have seen his organizational strength and asked him for help.

Another example of how these two styles interact can be seen in the lives of Neil, a judging organizer, and Sally, a perceiving organizer. One of Neil's chief complaints was that Sally never finished what she started. She had a closet full of needlepoint projects at various stages of completion, and she recently had bought another one.

The real contention between them, however, revolved around their grocery shopping excursions. When they came home, Neil carried the bags into the house and Sally started to put things away. "She at least gets the things into the freezer and the refrigerator now," Neil said, "but that's about all. And to be fair," he added, "that's a lot better than it used to be." What happened next at Sally and Neil's house was what usually happens with a perceiving person; the essentials were finished, so Sally decided to grab the magazine she had bought and sit down and read it.

"The rest can wait," Sally said. "Nothing's going to spoil. I'll get to it, but first I want to relax a moment."

But that moment often became a half hour or so. After the first fifteen minutes, Neil began to feel pressured to clean up the mess. And he was usually done when Sally finally walked into the kitchen.

During one of our counseling sessions Sally turned to Neil and said, "You're such a martyr. You have to put everything away even though I've told you I will finish! But no, you have to be one-up on me and finish before I can get back to it."

I called for a time out. "See how both of you are acting true to your personality types? Sally isn't really being lazy, and Neil isn't really being a martyr," I pointed out. "Sally can let things go for a while and do something else quite comfortably, but you, Neil, need to get things finished so you can relax." Neil just couldn't let anything sit there and enjoy whatever else he wanted to do; the unfinished task would keep nagging at him until it was done.

You might think that only judging people are perfectionists. The truth is that both types struggle with perfectionism. Perceiving organizers think they're great organizers, but if you ask them whether they can keep their files organized, they have to reply no. They are always in a hurry to get on to something else so they don't keep their things organized. These people often feel overwhelmed. They're always playing "catch up." Judging people are practicing perfectionists, and perceiving people are procrastinating perfectionists. For instance, Sally described how she struggled with her closet. She always was working on organizing it. One day, she got everything just the way she wanted it. She couldn't wait to show it to Neil. And he was truly impressed, it looked great.

They got into a fight, however, when he walked out of the closet and saw the "piles" of things that didn't fit into the closet, lying on the bedroom floor. Neil made the mistake of asking Sally what she intended to do with them. He was afraid that as soon as someone came to visit, the piles would quickly go back into the closet again, and all of Sally's work would go down the drain. Of course he forgot that Sally never did claim to be able to maintain the closet, she was simply "always organizing it."

Neil finally understood that as a perceiving person Sally basically had a play ethic about life, and he didn't have to make it his job to change her. In fact, the more accepting he was of that part of her, the more responsible she was about the areas that were really important.

In the end, a celebration of our differences and an understanding of how they affect us in our relationship can make it a winning situation for everyone. And that is going to help us get closer to each other.

Take a moment now to note each of your tendencies in the spaces below:

When I am organizing my world, I tend to be a (*J*, judging; *P*, perceiving) _____ organizer.

When my spouse is organizing the world, my mate tends to be a (*J*, judging; *P*, perceiving) _____ organizer.

Now write down all four of your and your mate's preferences from each of the last four chapters in the spaces below. In the first space, you will have either an *E* (extravert) or an *I* (introvert). In the second space, you will have either an *S* (sensing) or an *N* (intuitive). In the third space, you will have either a *T* (thinking) or an *F* (feeling). In the last space, you will have either a *J* (judging) or a *P* (perceiving).

My preference in all four personality traits is:

_____   _____   _____   _____

My spouse's preference in all four personality traits is:

_____   _____   _____   _____

Now that you have combined all four personality traits, we will look at your dominant process, the overriding aspect of your personality.

7

Living Together with Our Different Personalities

PROBABLY THE MOST central theme in Jan's and my conflicts has had to do with how I take everything so personally. "It's impossible to have even a fair fight with you," Jan says. That's because I usually go into a little routine that drives her crazy. When I sense she is upset about something, I begin to probe, trying to find out what the problem is. (We mentioned this in Chapter 5.) Then, Jan gets quiet and turns it all off. She says, "I just don't want to talk about it right now!"

That's my signal. It stirs up my personalizing personality, which automatically assumes that whatever the problem is, it's my fault. Now I'm offended, and my next comment to her shows that.

"Why do you always take everything so personally?" Jan asks. "You're just trying to make me feel guilty. Before I was only angry about [fill in the blank], but now I'm angry with you! When are you ever going to learn that I need you to show me some empathy and understanding when I'm upset? I don't want you to jump in and try to fix it or think it's always you!" She leaves the room, but eventually she returns to say, "Let's get this thing settled right here and now!"

Then an interesting thing happens, which Jan says is the real stinger. I become dogmatic and turn the argument around, making it all her fault. "I was just trying to help you. Don't you see that?" I ask. Then, angry, I list all the times in the past that she has responded this way. And the argument escalates as we both blame each other.

Does this sound familiar?

In the last four chapters, we have looked at the personality traits you and your spouse prefer. Now, we will look at the combinations formed by those four traits, using the letters you noted at the end of the last chapter, to help you determine more about who you really are. One of these four traits or functions will be your dominant process—the largest room, you might say, in your personality "house." This largest room will be represented by one of the two middle letters. Before we help you identify your dominant process, take a minute to write out again the four letters that you came up with from the previous chapters.

My preference in all four personality traits is:

_____   _____   _____   _____

My spouse's preference in all four personality traits is:

_____   _____   _____   _____

Our dominant process will come from the two sets of functions that are related to our observation style—the sensing (*S*) or the intuitive (*N*)—and our decision-making style—the thinking (*T*) or the feeling (*F*). The *S, N, T,* and *F* are referred to as functions of the personality, and they indicate how we take in information and the methods we then use to make critical decisions from that information. You will remember that they answer the questions "How do I take in information about my world?" and "How do I make decisions about my world?" (If you want a more detailed explanation of how the dominant process is determined, see Appendix 1.)

One of these four functions will be dominant—that is, it will be the most comfortable place in your personality house. We will give each dominant function the name of an animal or bird to help you remember them. You can find your dominant function on the Dominant Function circle below.

My Dominant Function

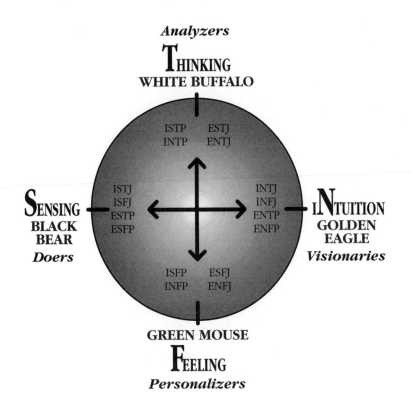

The Importance of the Dominant Process

Each of us will react to certain situations in rather predictable ways, according to the dominant process of our personality. This dominant process gives us many clues as to how we work, play, handle conflict in our relationship with each other, make choices, and, especially, solve problems. It has been one of the most helpful concepts for Jan and me to understand behaviors that otherwise could be very hurtful. It also helps us to know the areas that are extremely sensitive to each of us—places we need to stay away from if we want to deal effectively with our problems. As we look at the four dominant processes, think in terms of the animals we have used to label them as a way to better understand your own behavior and that of your spouse.

Dominant Sensing People

Black Bears

The people whose dominant decision-making process is the sensing function have the following combination of personality traits. Check the one that applies to you or to your spouse if one of your combinations is listed below:

_____ ESFP
_____ ESTP
_____ ISFJ
_____ ISTJ

As you can see by the letters, the sensing trait is present in each of these combinations. That trait is the key to understanding these personalities. Two of these combinations are extraverts and two are introverts. You won't easily notice some of these character-istics in introverted personalities, but if the introverts will let you see into their inner worlds, you will dis-cover that they are really dominant sensing people. All of these personalities reflect their sensing function by their comments. They might say:

- "Just give me the facts!"
- "Let's get it done now!"
- "You're wasting time!"
- "Let's be realistic about this!"

As you can see, dominant sensing people are the real "today" people. They live in the now, with the past and the future only distant concerns. In our semi-nars, we sometimes call these dominant sensing peo-ple black bears. Think about that analogy for a mo-ment. Have you ever seen a black bear wait for anything? If it wants what the picnickers are enjoying, it just lumbers in, scares everyone away, and eats the goodies. When people act this way, we often say things like, "Wow, he sure is a bear this morning!" or "You don't have to be such a bear about it."

Dominant sensing people are down-to-earth, prac-tical people. They have difficulty setting and articulat-ing goals since they think it is meaningless to look too far ahead. If you press them to look into the future, it may look bleak and pessimistic to them, so they would much rather spend their energy on today.

Sensing people are the doers. One of Jan's best friends is a dominant sensing person. When she helped us repaint some rooms in a house, she fin-ished more than twice what anyone else did in the same length of time. She is a doer.

The strengths of dominant sensing people are:

- Ability to work hard
- Enjoy the present
- Gifted in gathering information
- Are the "Doers"
- Trust the known
- Like measurable outcomes
- Good with tools
- Drive task through to completion

If you live with a dominant sensing person, a black bear, you need to know how this person handles conflict. Bears are the only ones who genuinely want to deal with problems, as long as the problems look solvable, since they don't want conflict to destroy their present moment. They will often assign blame quickly, saying, "This is your fault for these reasons. . . ." But they may just as easily say, "This is my fault for these reasons. . . ." They are more concerned about solving the problem than arguing about the blame. Usually, when they say it is your fault, and they have good reasons, you might as well agree. Once you agree and the problem is solved, it is forgotten. Dominant sensing people seldom hold grudges, for that would ruin their "now" as well.

If you do not agree with a sensing person's analysis of the problem, or want to dig deeper into the roots of the problem, he or she can become quite agitated in his or her desire to resolve the conflict. The sensing person may get physical, banging the table to make a point. Bears have been known to press and press in order to resolve a problem, but if there is no response, a strange sort of thing will occur. Suddenly, the problem is gone.

The black bear switches from using his dominant function to using its opposite function—the intuitive function. Carl Jung, the Swiss psychiatrist who first observed these traits in people, called this opposite function our "inferior function." Intuition is the least developed trait in dominant sensing people. It does not even appear in the four letters describing their personalities. When black bears are pushed to the wall—to the point of complete frustration—they will stop using the dominant function (the sensing function) and begin to use the opposite function (the intuitive). When they use this inferior function they become childish, extra sensitive, and very defensive.

Dominant sensing people will drop the subject. They act as if it all never really happened. When pressed by the other person, who probably is now ready to work things out, black bears are likely to say something like, "What problem? There's no problem here. There's nothing to talk about—absolutely nothing!" And they mean it! For these people, it is as if the problem never existed. They won't acknowledge it because it is messing up their "today."

The problem is that the problem still exists! And now they won't talk about it. If you are married to a black bear, the best way to handle this situation is to make certain that you deal with the problem *before* it gets to this point. And if you are a black bear it is important to recognize the limits of your frustration and anger. When you feel like walking out, stop and take a few minutes to regroup. Otherwise, like any one of us who falls into our inferior function, you will do and say things that can be very hurtful to the relationship. We all need to recognize that when we are acting in our inferior function, we are out of control.

Black bears are also very sensitive about the intuitive part of their personalities. When others criticize them for their lack of vision, for not seeing the bigger picture, or for not being able to quickly grasp some theoretical concept, it's as if a knife were being plunged into their souls. They get deeply hurt.

These are the limitations of the black bear:

- Tends to view things simplistically
- Becomes locked in to solutions that no longer work
- Has trouble seeing the big picture
- Tends to rush in order to finish
- Doesn't like to look very far into the future

These are the danger areas for sensing people. Be careful what you say about the lack of these attributes in their personalities.

Dominant Intuitive People

Golden Eagles

The person whose dominant process is the intuitive function has the following combination of personality traits. Check the one that applies to you or your spouse if one of your combinations is listed below:

_____ ENFP
_____ ENTP
_____ INFJ
_____ INTJ

Dominant intuitive people are the opposites of dominant sensing people; intuitives pay little attention to today and love to live for tomorrow. For them, today is but a stepping-stone to the future. We sometimes refer to intuitive people as golden eagles, because the eagle lives way up in the sky, scanning the horizon to see what it needs, anticipating the next catch. Even when the eagle lands, it stays way above everything, ready to catch the wind and fly away again.

When we are frustrated with people who are eagles we may say things like, "Wow, he is sure flighty today. I can't pin him down." (Being pinned down means being limited to today.) We might also say, "She sure has her head in the clouds today. When is she going to come down to earth so that we can take care of things?"

Intuitive people are dreamers, like the Man of La Mancha who was always dreaming of what could be. Brainstorming is one of their favorite activities. They could dream up ideas all day long. When done with that, they will set up a five- or ten-year plan. Whether they get around to doing it is secondary; creating it is fulfilling.

The strengths of the golden eagles are:

- Deal easily with symbols and the abstract
- Love to brainstorm new ideas and solutions
- See the bigger picture
- Able to anticipate the future
- Focus on imagination and discovery
- See what isn't obvious
- Quickly find the bottom line
- Reach for new possibilities

It's difficult to get golden eagles to consider the needs of the "now." It's easy to see, then, that their attitude toward problems and conflict is to "fly away," to avoid the conflict. They may get up and walk outside when right in the middle of a tense discussion. They may go for a ride or a walk. They may turn on the television while you're talking. Or they may fall sound asleep! You can almost see them pull down the shades behind their eyes and shut out everything that's unpleasant.

The attitude of the dominant intuitive toward a problem may be to "sleep on it." Their hope is that while they are asleep something will happen to resolve the problem, and they won't have to trouble themselves with it. In a marriage, intuitive people can be ever optimistic, unless they are depressed. "It'll all work out" is usually their motto. They live in an ideal world where problems don't exist, at least not for very long. But depression is always a threat to golden eagles. Their idealism sets them up for it.

If conflict continues and golden eagles have already tried to ignore it or shut down, they begin to use their inferior function. The trait that is the opposite of intuition is sensing, so when intuitive people have to face ongoing conflict, they start to act like black bears. Now they want to deal with things. They may even begin to pound the table to make their point, but when they do, something usually breaks. An eagle doesn't do a very good job imitating a bear!

If you are dealing with an eagle, a way to resolve a problem is to place the situation out in the future: "Let's brainstorm some ideas about how we might be able to resolve this issue sometime in the future." Here we are using the strength of the eagle—future thinking—to help intuitive people work on a problem that exists now. If you are an eagle, it is important to learn to recognize how you feel when you are reaching your breaking point. Rather than storming back into the situation after you have shut it off, try to use your creative energy to think of options to resolve the problem. One eagle that we know memorized this statement: "I'm ready to come back now. Can you give me thirty minutes to gather my thoughts?"

Jan is a golden eagle. Over the years we have

found ourselves laughing at the very things that before caused us much frustration. I can't always do it, but many times, when Jan shuts down and won't talk, I say to myself, *There she goes again, being an eagle.* Sometimes I say it out loud, and it breaks the impasse. We both laugh.

Just as black bears are sensitive about their inferior function, so also intuitive people are sensitive about their inferior function (the factual). You deeply wound intuitive people by pointing out their inability to be practical, their lack of attention to detail, or their inability to get things done on time. Other limitations of the golden eagles are:

- Uncomfortable with routine
- Lack realism in dealing with problems
- May read too much into things
- Difficulty making decisions when there are too many alternatives
- Miss the present

Dominant Thinking People

White Buffaloes

Dominant thinking people have the following combination of personality traits. Check the one that applies to you or your spouse if one of your combinations is listed below:

_____ ENTJ
_____ ESTJ
_____ INTP
_____ ISTP

These people are the dominant thinkers in our culture, the analyzers. They can make sense out of all kinds of numbers and facts. We are in awe of them and in many ways stay out of their way. We sometimes refer to dominant thinking people as white buffaloes. Have you ever said, "He's really got me buffaloed!" If you've been "buffaloed," you have been confronted by a dominant thinking person.

In his book *Centennial,* James Michener describes how the Indians viewed the white buffalo. They were in awe of this rare beast, thinking it possessed unique powers. The Indians never killed white buffaloes because they were afraid of them. Many times we think of dominant thinkers in the same way—we are intimidated by their ability to analyze.

White buffaloes are fascinated by facts. Whether it is buying a car or figuring out a way to get their computer to pay the bills, they will gather every piece of information they can find, organize what they have collected, and then analyze it carefully before they make a decision. They love *Consumer Reports* magazine.

Dominant thinking people have a great ability to be objective in any situation or to sum up a discussion by organizing it into three main points with a few subpoints. They are gifted with an ability to pull things together in a logically sound way.

White buffaloes are strong in the following areas:

- Able to analyze the flaws or problems in things
- Able to see how parts relate to whole
- Come to conclusions quickly
- Can see the logical consequences of choices
- Seek fairness and justice
- Able to critically assess work done by others
- Use time—past, present, and future—related to tasks
- Able to see the logical flow of ideas and projects

White buffaloes lack the empathic warmth, however, that could really make their arguments convincing. When it comes to handling conflict, they act as if they are interested in solving a problem, but in reality, their primary interest is in "analyzing" the problem. If you are married to a white buffalo, you can expect a constant flow of questions in search of more information as you discuss a problem. Often, once you get over being "buffaloed," you may, in frustration, say something like, "All you want to do is talk about the problem. You never want to do anything about it." And then the buffalo wants to analyze what you meant by that statement!

Buffaloes have great memories, but they usually remember only what is useful. I remember listening to a white buffalo tell me about a recent sales trip with his sales manager, who hadn't traveled with him for eight years. Throughout their trip, this man kept telling his sales manager what they had done together eight years before, whom they had called on, who had bought what, and even what they had for meals. Needless to say, his sales manager was impressed by his attention to detail. The white buffalo had remembered the useful details of that earlier trip.

But watch out! A current problem could recur in conversation three years from now, and the dominant thinking person will say something like, "You know, we went through this same thing three years ago. Is this going to happen every three years?"

If dominant thinking people get pushed too far, they will eventually fall into their inferior function (the feeling function). When they do this, they will probably get very emotional—not in a healthy way, but in a reactive way. They may even apologize and get romantic. Buffaloes are the only ones who will capitulate in an argument. But when they do, you need to be very careful. That's really not the end of it. Instead, this conflict has just become another piece of data that may prove useful somewhere in the future. Remember, the buffalo never forgets.

Your best response to their apology is to accept it, and then go back to your discussion of the problem once they have calmed down. If you are the buffalo, it is important for you to learn to analyze your own process. Write out the issues from the last couple of conflicts you've been involved in. Look carefully at what took place before and after you gave in. This will help you to see what sets you off and pushes you into your inferior function.

The following list shows some of the limitations of the white buffaloes:

- Appear cold and indifferent
- Uncomfortable with own feelings
- Difficulty in building relationships
- Can make decisions too quickly
- Cannot read other people's feelings; lack tact

Comments on the white buffalo's lack of emotion or lack of tact or empathy, or statements like "You must have ice in your veins" are difficult for the dominant thinking person to forget. Again, it is best to develop ways to deal with conflict before it forces the white buffaloes into their inferior feeling process.

Dominant Feeling People

Green Mice

Dominant feeling people have the following combination of personality traits. Check the one that applies to you or your spouse if one of your combinations is listed below:

_____ ENFJ
_____ ESFJ
_____ INFP
_____ ISFP

When the feeling function is dominant, the person is a "personalizer." This person experiences life intensely and takes everything very personally. We sometimes refer to this person as a green mouse. If a buffalo walked through the mouse's territory and broke some blades of grass, the mouse would wonder, "Why did that buffalo do that to me?"

Some of the strengths of green mice are:

• Can grasp the emotional tone of the whole picture
• Make personal values a high priority
• Promote harmony and reconciliation
• Give personal meaning to ideas and situations
• Able to persuade
• Able to empathically understand others
• Value other people's feelings
• Brings warmth and enthusiasm to groups and events

Green mice mark their territory. They know every burrow, every blade of grass, every flower, and every weed in their space. Nothing escapes them. Mice are the real "nesters." They take care to protect their homes and their families. They work hard at home and at work to build a strong sense of connectedness between people.

Yet, when there is a conflict, the dominant feeling person's first concern seems to be everyone else. These people are always trying to calm things down by explaining what everyone else meant in the situation. Sometimes they are even accused of defending the enemy in their efforts to help others understand why someone did (or didn't do) something. I am a green mouse, and I have been accused of defending the enemy when all I was trying to do was "fix" Jan's feelings by explaining the motives of the other person. I was convinced that if she could only understand why someone said what he did or acted in a certain way, she wouldn't be so upset. Needless to say, it has never worked.

If an argument gets a little loud, the feeling spouse's first concern will not be the two of you, but someone else: "Please don't wake the kids," or "Don't let the neighbors hear." It's not that he or she is trying to protect an image; the green mouse just doesn't want to upset anyone else.

Green mice often internalize the tension they feel from trying to keep everyone happy. They get tightness in their neck, headaches, or a sensitive stomach. They don't know how to turn off their caring, and they have great difficulty focusing on themselves, or even their spouses.

When green mice get pushed too far, they resort to their inferior function (the thinking process). It is amazing to watch green mice trying to act like intimidating white buffaloes, but that is exactly what they do. Suddenly, in the midst of the argument, they loudly summarize the logic of their point of view. In their frustration, they may make dogmatic assertions, such as, "You never . . ." or "You always . . ." Since their logic comes from their inferior function, it is a very personal logic and seldom makes much sense to an objective observer.

One must be very careful not to criticize the feeling spouse's logic, since this is where he or she is most vulnerable, sensitive, and defensive. I am a hopeless personalizer. Jan really hurts me, for instance, when she is critical of my logic or if she teases me about the illogical way I give directions. (I use "landmarks" instead of street names, like "a big white house with a rocking chair on the porch.") She doesn't have to tell me—I know—my logic is not my strength.

The limitations of the green mice are:

- Have difficulty confronting others
- Personalize everything, even logic
- Tend to ignore things that would disrupt harmony
- Easily become caretakers
- Can become too caught up in the emotions of the moment

We've looked at the dominant part of our personalities. All of this is clearly seen in those people who are extraverts. But it's a little more complex in those of us who are introverts.

You Won't Always Meet the Dominant Personality Trait

As we all know, people are complicated. Just when we think we've figured someone out, the person does something that seems to be completely out of character, and that sends us guessing about him or her again. We mentioned the mystery of personhood. Some of this mystery is what makes living with another person so challenging—yet fascinating.

Myers and Briggs noted an exception to the dominant process. People who are introverts don't show their dominant trait when we first meet them. In fact, it may take years before they let us see that part of them. Myers and Briggs pointed out that when you meet an introvert, you meet his or her aide. The general—the dominant process—is in the command tent. Introverts might invite you to meet the general once they get to know you, but again they might not. They hide who they truly are.

For example, I am a green mouse, as I mentioned earlier. My four letters are *INFP*. That means that my general—my dominant process—is the feeling function (the *F*). Yet I express this primarily in my inner world. When I meet you, you will not see this part of me; my general is busy working in the tent. What you will see is my auxiliary process—my general's aide— the intuitive process. You will probably think I am a quiet golden eagle, since that's what shows. But when you get to know me, you'll meet my general—and he's a green mouse!

You may be surprised by my introverted part. A lot of people who know me think of me as an extravert. But they are responding to skills I have learned over the years in leading groups and learning how to socialize with people. As we said earlier, introverts are much more mysterious and, therefore, more difficult to figure out.

We know a thirty-year-old corporate executive with a Fortune 500 company who was nicknamed "The Young Turk" by his business associates—a headstrong wheeler-dealer who played all the corporate power games. Yet the man always maintained that no one in the company knew his real personality. "I'm really very quiet. Ask my wife. She'll tell you that she runs our home and our social life." This man's wife was one of the few people who saw him as he really was, an introvert who had a very private inner world. He was an *ISTJ*.

Extraverts, however, relate to the outer world. They usually show you right away who they are. Jan's that way. She meets people easily and asks something about them—and may tell them something about herself. (Remember the two of us sitting in that fogbound airport waiting room.) So when you meet an extravert, you meet their general. Jan is an extraverted golden eagle. When you meet her, you will see her dominant intuitive function, which is her general.

The key to whether or not you are seeing a person's true personality is whether or not that person is extraverted or introverted. Remember, if you are living with an introvert, it is always a two-stage process. First, you meet the aide, and then maybe later you will meet the general who is in the tent.

Living Together

How do these personalities survive living together? One of the more difficult combinations is when one partner's dominant function is the other person's inferior function. A sensing black bear living with an intuitive golden eagle, or a thinking white buffalo living with a feeling green mouse, need to be careful with each other. Each knows the other person's weakest part too well, because each knows his strength is the weakness of the other. The partners in these relationships can say and do things that can destroy their relationship. They need to be careful to stay away from their own inferior function. It's not that they can't live together—they just need to be careful about issues related to their respective inferior functions.

For example, Jerry is a black bear, and Jenny is a golden eagle. In the early years of their marriage, they were always at odds about issues that were related to their personality differences. Each thought the other was simply doing things to be irritating. Jenny thought it was ridiculous that Jerry couldn't sit down with her and set some goals for their family. She wanted one-year goals, five-year goals, and some longer-term goals. Jerry got defensive every time she brought up this long-range planning. Finally, out of frustration, he took the offensive and started to tease her about her need to live in tomorrow.

"What's the matter with you?" he asked. "Why can't you just enjoy today? Tomorrow may never come. You've got to get your head out of the clouds and come back down to earth!"

That just set Jenny off. "You're so short-sighted you can't see beyond your nose!" she told him in no uncertain terms. "You don't know how to plan for anything. If it wasn't for me, you wouldn't have a thing. There's more to life than today!" she added.

These statements may seem harsh to you, but to Jerry and Jenny they were more than harsh—they were a direct attack on each other's inferior function. One could say they really knew how to hurt each other. So it is especially important for these combinations to understand their own and their spouse's weaknesses and strengths and to tread carefully around the weaknesses.

My inferior function is (either sensing or intuitive; thinking or feeling) _____.

My spouse's inferior function is _____.

Look one more time at the Dominant Function chart on page 119. Then, let's look at some of the positive things we can do in order to live together with our individual personality types and find a growing and deepening intimacy.

Resolving Conflict Between Personality Types

As we have said earlier, Jan is an intuitive golden eagle and I am a feeling green mouse. When we face problems or conflict in our marriage, we usually react in a way that is typical to our personalities. Jan's tendency is to "fly away," as we mentioned at the beginning of this chapter. And I personalize everything. How did we learn to get beyond these natural responses so we could work through the issues?

We have found a simple, four-step process for resolving problems that we've illustrated on page 138. The process involves the use of all four dominant functions—the sensing function, the intuitive function, the thinking function, and the feeling function— beginning with the sensing function. People who are dominant sensing love to collect data. If we are going to resolve a problem, we need to gather information.

Let's say that our problem is that our checkbook is always out of balance and our account is overdrawn. To solve this problem, we need to know why it happens. Is it because we spend too much? Or are we just too busy and preoccupied to get to the bank and make our deposits? What actually is the problem behind this problem? A dominant sensing person (the black bear), who, by the way, makes a great accountant, will love digging through our check records, coming up with a description of our income and our spending, and clearly identifying the problem. (If your spouse is a black bear, let him or her perform this part of the process.) For the sake of illustration, let's say that after looking at the data, we see that the problem is that we spend too much.

The second step in resolving our problem is to brainstorm all possible solutions, a dominant intu-

Problem Solving

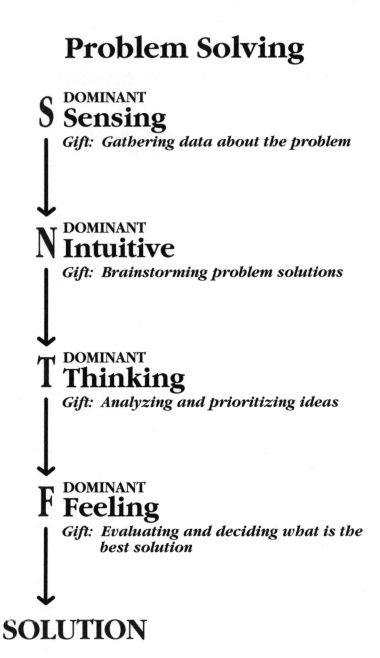

S DOMINANT
Sensing
Gift: Gathering data about the problem

N DOMINANT
Intuitive
Gift: Brainstorming problem solutions

T DOMINANT
Thinking
Gift: Analyzing and prioritizing ideas

F DOMINANT
Feeling
Gift: Evaluating and deciding what is the best solution

SOLUTION

itive's dream. "Let's sit down and think of every possible way we can either cut back on our spending or increase our income," a golden eagle may say. Ideas may include anything from selling all and moving to the woods to getting a second job—write down and consider every idea. Set a time limit on this, or the intuitive person (the golden eagle) will never get around to resolving the problem. He can brainstorm all day.

The third step is to objectively analyze all the possible ideas generated in step two. This is the gift of the dominant thinking person, the white buffalo. He or she can take all of the ideas generated by the intuitive and prioritize them. Selling everything and moving to the country might be tossed out as being undesirable. Getting a second job might be considered, as might selling a car and getting a cheaper one. Every possibility is looked at, with the best ideas ranked according to their objective possibilities. (If one of you is a white buffalo, this third step should be assigned to him or her.)

The fourth step is to subjectively analyze what we have ranked as a result of step three. This is the domain of the dominant feeling person, the green mouse. Here, the green mouse looks at what the buffalo has prioritized and evaluates and decides what is the best solution. Perhaps the car has some special meaning to one of us, so we cross that off the list for now. We decide on a second job for a period of time as our solution to the problem, along with budgeting ourselves carefully to reduce our spending. We decide based on what feels like something we can successfully do and how it will affect us emotionally. The green mouse is excellent at this task.

Usually, a couple, using both their dominant and inferior functions, will be able to cover all four areas used in the above four steps. The only function un-available to us is our inferior function, the opposite of our dominant function. For example, my dominant function is feeling, which makes my inferior function thinking. This means I still have available to me the sensing and intuitive functions, in addition to my feel-ing function. Jan's dominant function is the intuitive, which makes her inferior function the sensing. She can use her intuitive function, as well as her thinking and feeling functions. I have the sensing function Jan lacks, and Jan has the thinking function I lack. Thus, between us, we have access to all four functions needed for problem solving.

If you know that you both have the same inferior function, find someone who can help you there, for all four steps need to be followed for a successful resolution of the problem. For example, you both may be green mice, which means that neither one of you is good at the thinking function. It is important to find someone, preferably a white buffalo-type ac-countant, who will fill that gap in your problem-solv-ing skills.

A Warning

One important warning needs to be given here. Sometimes we find people using these personality traits as an excuse for the way they behave. "This is the way I am, and you had better just accept it," they say to their spouses. If you are feeling that way, you've missed the whole point of this section. The key is understanding. We want to understand how our spouse operates and what his or her personality is like. We also want our spouses to understand us bet-ter. But a sense of accommodation and compromise follows this understanding. I may be this way, but I ask myself, "What can I begin to learn to do that will make it better for both of us?" It's this kind of attitude that will help any personality combination become better partners in intimacy.

Now that we understand our personalities better—the part of us that isn't likely to change—let's look at the part of us that can be changed: the aspects of our behavior that have been influenced by our past experiences. We need to look at some of the baggage we bring to our relationships, which either enhances those relationships or hinders them from growing.

PART THREE

How Our Past Affects Our Ability to Love and Be Loved

8

The Destructive Traditions of Our Childhood Families

JAN'S AND MY families were quite different, at least the way we remember them and the way we experienced them. Jan grew up in a big house, across the street from the church, so every time a school choir or some guest speaker came, the logical place for them to stay was at her house. People were always around for meals and for overnight lodging. They felt free to "drop in" any time. Jan loved the interaction and activity. (You can see why she enjoyed that bus full of young people from that outreach program to Mexico who spent the day at our home.)

I can remember people coming for dinner at different times, but usually they came when they were invited, and it was all very formal and social. Even if we had company, I had to be there only for a while, and then I could leave. The attic of our house was finished off and became my room. It was large, and I loved it. I enjoyed my quiet isolation, knowing that I probably wouldn't be disturbed.

You can imagine what happened when Jan's ex-

pectations collided with mine. Jan remembers meal-
times as exciting, partly because you never knew who
might join you for a meal. I remember our kitchen
table with my dad and me on one side, my sister at
the end, and my mother on the other side. The other
end was pushed up against the kitchen window. We
sat that way for every meal; no one ever thought of
sitting somewhere different. The times someone else
ate with us, we ate in the dining room, and it felt
much more formal. Our family meal patterns were
only one of the differences we brought to our marriage from our families of origin.

We hadn't worked out these details prior to marriage, so we each obviously expected, "We'll do it the
way *I've* always done it." And when our differences
conflicted, we could seldom talk about it because we
weren't really aware of the issues. All we knew was
that one of us had to give in for there to be peace in
the marriage, a pattern guaranteed to block the
growth of closeness.

A minor confrontation occurred our first Christmas.
We decided to decorate the tree together. What a di-
saster! Jan gave me half of the icicles to put on one
side of the tree while she worked on her side. Jan put
icicles on the tree one at a time, just as her family had
done. (They, in fact, had put one on every needle!)
The trees at her house always had blue lights and
waves of silver icicles. When anyone walked by the
tree and made a breeze, some of those icicles would
stick to the other branches, so someone would
straighten them. Then, after Christmas her family took
the icicles off, one by one!

In my family we were much more casual about
decorating the Christmas tree. We'd take a few icicles
and toss them on the tree. Needless to say, I finished
hanging my icicles much sooner than Jan did.

Jan came around to look at my side of the tree and was first astounded, and then angry. "Look at what you've done," she cried. My side looked so terrible to her that she spent the next half hour straightening it. I never quite got over the rejection!

No one escapes the influence of the past. Even though we want to believe we are free to act any way we want, determined to break out of the mold, we are actually driven by patterns we repeat time after time. Family history, early behavior, birth order, and the general home environment all contribute in a profound and critical way to the shaping of who we are and the way we relate.

Family History

One of the most powerful influences on our lives is our family history, as the story of Jerry illustrates. When Jerry was twelve years old, his father had an affair, left Jerry's mother, and married the other woman. Jerry's father spent a minimal amount of time with Jerry. Jerry was hurt, humiliated, and angry with his father. As an adult, his relationship with his father was very limited because of his strong feelings about what his father had done to himself and his mother.

I did not hear this story from Jerry. His wife related it to me as she sat in my office alone. Their oldest son was twelve, and Jerry had just informed her that he loved someone else and wanted to marry her. When his wife confronted him with the parallel between what he was doing and what his father had done, Jerry told her angrily, "That's in the past! It has nothing to do with what I'm doing! Don't ever bring that up again."

It didn't help Jerry's wife to know that her story was

not an isolated one, but was, in reality, all too common. Patterns repeat themselves over the generations. Our family history affects each of us, and the more we try to ignore it, bury it, or wish it away, the more it affects us. The past always presses for expression in the present.

The Family Is a System

One of the main reasons our families have such a powerful effect upon each of us is that they operate as a system. And as a system, each family seeks to maintain sameness, or homeostasis. What does this mean?

To define the family as a system means that it is an entity unto itself and resists any kind of outside influence. If someone in a family wants to change, the family will work extra hard to find ways to neutralize those changes. I remember a young woman who had been hospitalized several times for severe depression. Each time, after a period of treatment, she would improve enough to be sent home.

Several months later, she would be readmitted for depression again. This had happened three times. On her fourth admission, someone insisted that the counselors investigate her family background. The social worker found that she had been blamed for a tragedy that had happened in the family some years earlier.

Her family needed a scapegoat, someone to be a problem so that no one needed to look at the real problem. She somehow had been given this role in her family, and after she broke out of that role in the hospital, her family unconsciously put pressure on her to be the "sick" one in the family when she came home. After her final hospital stay, the social workers helped her find a new place to live, away from the family, and she was able, finally, to break the cycle.

Why would a family want someone to be "sick"? To understand a closed system, consider the heating unit in your home. It consists of a thermostat and a furnace. Imagine that somehow the thermostat is set at 90 degrees, and it's in one of those locked cases, so you can't change the setting. When you come home, it's hot! It's also the middle of December and cold outside, so you quickly open a window to cool off your house. As the cold air begins to circulate in the house and starts to give you some relief, the thermostat senses that the temperature is dropping below the set point, so it sends a message to the furnace to begin heating up the house.

Since you can't get to the thermostat to reset it, the furnace will blow hot air into your house. At the same time, you have the windows open so that cold air is coming in from outside. The furnace knows only one thing to do. It must maintain the temperature inside the house at 90 degrees, and it will destroy itself in the process of trying to achieve that task.

In the same way, families will literally destroy themselves in an effort to keep everything the same and, at the same time, verbally affirm their desire to change. And the family thermostat is hidden away in the unconscious beyond our direct control, making it difficult to adjust or change. This inability to change makes a family dysfunctional.

There's a lot of talk about dysfunctional families, so much so that Rich Capperella, a radio announcer on a Los Angeles station, declared after California's 1991 elections that Proposition 222 (banning the use of the words *dysfunctional* and *codependency* in public gatherings) had passed the referendum. I laughed at his joke (there was no Prop 222), as I recognized how tired of those words we can get.

All of us come from dysfunctional families because we all are human beings and we all sin. My present family is dysfunctional. Your present family is too. The family I grew up in was dysfunctional. The family you grew up in was too. Some families are just more destructive in their dysfunction than others.

With everything that is being said about dysfunctional families, one could easily be led to believe that dysfunctional families are a problem unique to our day and age. But destructive families go back to the beginning of time, to the days recorded in the Old Testament. Let's look at a well-known dysfunctional family of that time: the family begun by Abraham and Sarah and carried on by Isaac and Rebekah. As we do so, decide if you agree when we say they were dysfunctional.[1]

Twin boys, Jacob and Esau, were born to Isaac and Rebekah, whose lives seemed to be ideal prior to the twins' arrival. Isaac and Rebekah's love was "love at first sight." And we might imagine that their lives continued in this idyllic pattern until the boys came along. (Quite typical, isn't it?)

But Isaac came from a very disturbed family, even though the apostle Paul describes Isaac's father, Abraham, as the model of our faith. This Old Testament family passed their problems down from generation to generation, just as we do today. We will follow their story as we talk about the mechanisms that keep us stuck in destructive cycles. We call these patterns "destructive traditions."

Maintaining the Traditions

Four destructive traditions lock families into a pattern that repeats from generation to generation. Families exercise control over their members through family myths, family secrets, circular communication, and family roles.

As we talk about these four destructive traditions, don't begin by thinking about your present family. You are probably too close to it. (That's your kids' job when they go into therapy sometime in the future!) Look, instead, at the family of your childhood. (There's one exception to this. If your children are grown, you might be far enough removed from the immediate problems to objectively look at your own family.)

Family Myths

We remain stuck in the same destructive family patterns because we hold on to family myths. These myths are *something the family talks about but never does*. One of the most common myths, which we hear almost every time we ask about someone's family, is "We're very close," or "Our family is really there for each other."

We've talked with people about their families after they state this, and they go on to tell us how separated and distant the family members really are from one another. But they usually end the discussion by repeating the words, "But we're really close as a family." It's almost as if they were unaware of what they had just been telling us.

One patient in our hospital program, a former professional baseball player, told us, "Yeah, my brothers are there for me when I need them." He described his brothers and his mom and dad, and he said nothing negative about them. They were perfect brothers, perfect parents. They owned a cabin together, he said, and enjoyed going there together to fish.

We didn't say anything in response. Instead, we waited to see what he might discover in the next weeks, as he continued to look at his issues.

Two weeks later this tough athlete admitted, "I haven't had a visit from anyone, not from my parents or one of my brothers. Not even a phone call." Then he described the real picture of his family. His parents were divorced, and his dad was remarried. They were still very antagonistic toward each other. "The only thing that holds my family together is that cabin—and we fight about it all the time," he said.

"But I thought you told me that your family was close," I replied.

"I did, but we're not."

Family myths have existed from the beginning of history. Scripture doesn't say anything directly about the family myths in Jacob and Esau's family, but we can imagine what they might have been. One of the myths that must have been believed by the descendants of Abraham was that they were a very spiritual family.

We can readily see how this myth got started. If Abraham was your grandfather, the man to whom God said, "I will make you a great nation. I will bless you and make your name great," the man to whom God spoke time and time again, it would be reasonable to think that your family was spiritual. Certainly, the people who lived at that time and watched Abraham and Isaac prosper under God's care thought this family knew God intimately. The apostle Paul referred to Abraham as the father of our faith, the one who taught us what faith was all about. But all wasn't what it appeared to be.

In Hebrews 11, the faith chapter, Abraham takes up almost a third of the chapter. But Isaac is passed over quickly. He is mentioned only in that he blessed both of his sons. His faith and spirituality were not like his father's, even though we may think he was as spiritual because he was Abraham's son and shared in the promise. Isaac's spirituality was, in fact, probably very weak or absent.

Jacob didn't seem to inherit his grandfather's faith either. (The saying "God doesn't have any grandchildren" certainly seemed to apply in this family.) We see evidence of this in Jacob's stealing his brother's birthright.

Jacob put on Esau's clothes and a pair of gloves Rebekah made for him from the hairy skin of young goats so he would seem hairy like his brother. Then he went into his father's tent and approached the elderly Isaac, who was almost blind, saying, "I'm Esau, your son."

We can imagine the white-haired old man motioning to Jacob. "Come a little closer." Then Isaac felt Jacob's arms. *It feels like Esau,* Isaac thought to himself, *it even smells like him. But it sounds like Jacob.* Esau was the hunter, a sportsman; Jacob was a mommy's boy who probably was squeaky clean!

Suspicious, Isaac asked his son, "How did you find the game for the stew so quickly?"

And Jacob replied, "The Lord, your God, provided it."

There is an important little nuance here. (We read that text for years and never saw it.) Jacob doesn't say, "The Lord, *our* God, provided it." Instead, he says it's the Lord, Isaac's God. Why? Because Jacob didn't know the first thing about God. He left home soon after that, knowing practically nothing about the God of Abraham and Isaac, and Jacob spent the next twenty years learning about Him, learning the things he was never taught at home. The description of their family as a spiritual family was a myth based on the family's relationship to Abraham and to God's promise to them. Because there was so little spiritual vitality in this family, we can infer that one of their myths was "We're a spiritual family."

We all bring myths to our present relationships that are rooted in our families of origin. Sometimes the myth is similar to that held by Jacob and Esau's family —that we are a "spiritual" family. Sometimes the myth is that Mom is really sweet and gentle, even though, in reality, all she does is criticize us. The criticism, since it was covered by a myth, is ignored. It takes hard work to identify these myths and to break the hold they have on us and to see how they set us up for unrealistic expectations in our relationships. But the truth can and must be faced if we are to break free from the past in order to more fully enjoy the present.

Take a moment to think about your own childhood. Check the myths below that your family may have believed.

_____ "Our family was really close."
_____ "We were a spiritual family."
_____ "We were a happy family."
_____ "Everyone really cared about each other."
_____ "My family's there for me when I need them."
_____ "If I have a problem, the family will take care of it."
_____ (Write any other family myths you may have had.) ___

Family Secrets

We hear a lot about family secrets in alcoholic families, families with incest or abuse, and families with some other big problem they wish to hide from each other and the rest of the world. Mental illness in the family is often kept secret, for instance. One man told us, "As I was packing my things to come to the hospital, I felt as if my dead father was in the room. I could hear him saying, 'Family business stays family business.'"

He continued, "My mom has been in a mental hospital for over twenty years. When I was growing up, she would flip out and have to go into the hospital. While she was there, we would move so that when she came out no one in the neighborhood would know she had a problem. Then, when she had a relapse, Dad would move again. Finally, when she was committed for life, we didn't have to move anymore. But nobody ever talked about her illness, not even in the family. We each knew when we were supposed to visit her, but nobody ever said a word about her problem."

Mental illness, incest, abuse, and alcohol or drug addictions are all kept as family secrets. But these secrets include more than just these obviously damaging behaviors. Basically, a family secret is *something we do in our families, but never talk about*. It is the opposite of a family myth, which is something the family talks about but never does. Having family secrets can be compared with having a baby elephant in our living room; at a very young age, we learn to ignore the elephant. Eventually, the elephant gets larger, and so we put a doily and a lamp on it and consider it part of the furniture. As it gets larger, we can no longer use the living room, and even then, no one in the family asks why we have an elephant in there.

We go to a friend's house, and maybe he or she has a dead dog (their family's secret) lying on the living room floor. We somehow know not to ask why our friend keeps a dead dog there, or why he or she doesn't have an elephant in the living room as we do at our house. When we go home, we also learn not to ask any questions about why a dead dog is in our friend's living room. It's a secret. We learn how secrets work very early in life.

It may be that our elephant—our family secret—is that we never talk about or even admit to having bad feelings about anything. Family secrets operate to maintain the status quo in our disturbed families. The family secret in Isaac and Rebekah's family was the way their family was divided. That family had a coalition between Rebekah and Jacob and another coalition between Isaac and Esau, which actually was a reaction to the intense connection between Jacob and his mother. We could use words like *symbiotic* and *fusion* to describe their relationship.

If you want to see a Rebekah-Jacob type of relationship in action, read "Mama" in the cartoon section of your newspaper. This "Mama" is typical of the mother who's always manipulating her kids' lives— and the children are always trying to sabotage Mama's efforts by their passive resistance.

Rebekah saw her son, Jacob, as the model child who deserved his father's blessing. Isaac, however, saw Jacob as a wimpy little boy who stayed tied too close to Mama's apron strings. This boy probably *liked* to clean the tent. This boy *did* like to cook. Isaac probably thought, *That's not the way a son should be!*

Rebekah, on the other hand looked at Esau in an equally derogatory way. She probably thought, *I have so little in common with him. He's always camping out or hunting or fishing. And he's so dirty all the time. I'm going to invest my time in Jacob.*

That left Esau motherless, so Isaac made up for it by forming a close relationship with him. The two sides of the family became divided.

The two brothers, Esau and Jacob, were also at odds with each other. We can imagine their interaction the day Esau sold his birthright for a bowl of soup. Esau came home that day and smelled the delicious aroma of a wonderful soup cooking. He'd been hunting unsuccessfully for a couple of days, and he was famished. *I'm starving, and that smells so incredible,* he probably thought. He asked Jacob to give him some soup.

Instead of ladling out a portion to Esau, as most brothers would do, Jacob used this opportunity to manipulate his brother. *I've got him where I want him,* he said to himself. Then he replied, "Give me your birthright, and I'll give you some soup."

Esau naturally thought, *Well, what good is the birthright if I'm going to die of starvation?* So he agreed.

And Jacob gave Esau a bowl of soup, probably the most expensive bowl of soup that's ever been eaten. The birthright was sold, and the two brothers were divided.

What about that beautiful love relationship between Isaac and Rebekah? By the time the boys were teens, we suppose from the way the story unfolds, they probably were sleeping in separate tents.

The overriding secret in Isaac and Rebekah's family was that there was a big chasm between the two sides of the family.

Family secrets all too often are kept even from ourselves. One woman told us about a family secret that seemed almost unbelievable. When she was only ten years old her father moved to Florida to take a new job. He called and sent short notes every now and then, and her mother always said, "When Dad gets settled, we'll probably move there too."

A year after Dad moved, the girl and her mother went to visit him in Orlando, but they stayed at his friend's home, rather than in his apartment. That scenario went on for five years until a cousin mentioned "your parents' divorce" to the teenager.

Shocked, the girl confronted her mother, who at first denied it and then admitted that she had separated from her husband when the girl's dad moved away. They had tried to reconcile during that first visit, but were not able to resolve their problems, so they had divorced soon after that. Mom had never told the daughter. Dad had never told her, either. She had been living in a make-believe world! You can imagine how angry she was at her parents, who had lied to her for five years!

All of us have some family secrets, which are often difficult to identify. We have lived too long with a pattern of closing our eyes to these truths to be able to quickly put our finger on them. As a result, we bring them as baggage into our own relationships without even knowing what they are. They can infect our relationships and set up destructive patterns that we feel helpless to break.

Think about your own family of origin. Check the family secrets that existed there:

_____ "Our family never admitted to having bad feelings about anything."
_____ "Anger was denied in our family, even though Dad was a rageaholic."
_____ "One of my parents was an alcoholic, but no one ever admitted it."

_____ "My mother/sister is a lesbian, or my brother has AIDS."

_____ "Someone in our family has a problem with drugs."

_____ "One of my parents (or a relative) sexually abused me or a brother or sister."

_____ "One of my parents had an affair with another person."

_____ (Write out any of your other family secrets.) _____

Circular Communication

Family communication is a powerful issue. It is the strong link in passing on to the next generation the destructive patterns and traditions from which we want to be free. With circular communication, no one talks directly to anyone else about any kind of problem. Instead, family members use a "go-between." Cliff and Claire Huxtable, in "The Cosby Show," wouldn't know about circular communication. They talk directly to the persons they have a problem with, because they have the perfect family.

Here's how circular communication works. We can usually remember this happening in our own childhood. Dad often came home tired and irritable, so Mom would try to protect us from him. She would watch for his arrival, and then get us busy in our rooms with our homework or some other assignment so we would be out of Dad's way for a while. But if we happened to "be in the way" and catch the wrath of Dad, she would step between Dad and us and send us to our rooms while she helped to cool Dad down. Then she would come up to our rooms to explain how tired Dad was and how awful his boss was and that Dad really didn't mean to be so harsh with us. After that, she would go back downstairs to Dad and explain to him how sorry we were and that we really didn't mean to upset him and that, after all, the family was important so he needed to get over his anger at the kids. Finally she would go back upstairs to our rooms and tell us that Dad was sorry and that we could come back to the family room, but must keep it down for, after all, Dad really was tired.

We would gingerly come back into the family room without looking at Dad directly. Usually by now, he was into the news on the TV or was reading the paper, so he didn't really notice or acknowledge that we had come back into the room. Once he did, everything went on as if nothing had happened. A great example of circular communication. No one would talk directly to the one with whom they had a problem—it all went through Mom.

In the story of Jacob and Esau, the pattern of circular communication is seen in the events that follow Jacob's deception of his father. Esau held a grudge against Jacob and determined that once his father was dead he was going to kill Jacob. Now, he didn't go to Jacob and say, "I have a problem with you. You deceived me." Instead, he held it in and vowed to kill Jacob.

We read: "And the words of Esau her older son *were told* to Rebekah"[2]. Notice that it was not Esau who told her. We don't know who told her. Perhaps Esau told a friend, who told another friend, who told his mother, who told Rebekah. Somehow she found out, but it was by a circular means of communicating.

Now it is easy for us to continue this pattern. Often Mom continues to be the hub of communication in the family, or sometimes one of the siblings volunteers for the task. All information is funneled through that person as the hub within the family. It gives that person a lot of power and serves to perpetuate the destructive family patterns that we will in turn bring to our own relationships. The person at the hub, which is often Mom, can interpret what each side says and shade the meaning or add some new meaning. For instance, in the family situation we mentioned earlier, Dad might not have meant to apologize to the children, but Mom changed what he said to include an apology.

The communication problems between Isaac and Rebekah went beyond circular communication. There was little communication between the two of them. You would think, for instance, that Isaac would have at least made an offhand remark about Rebekah's manipulations as she set up the "blessing" event. But he didn't say a word.

If it had been the Huxtable family on TV, Cliff would have gathered the whole family together and confronted the deception. He would have said, "Okay, we've got a problem here." But then, functional families have always existed only on TV—the Cleavers, the Waltons, the Huxtables. And even then, they are few. We have to look hard to find good models for clear and direct communication.

In Isaac's case, he says and does nothing. A little later, when Rebekah heard that Esau was determined to kill Jacob once Isaac was dead, Rebekah went to Isaac with a phony suggestion that supposedly would protect Jacob from his brother. She said that Jacob needed a wife and the only good women were back in her hometown.

That was a great opportunity for Isaac to say, "Sit down, and let's talk a moment. What's the deal here? Were you behind this little scenario when Jacob stole the blessing from Esau?"

Yet not a word is said. Isaac just agrees, "Okay, let's send Jacob to your brother's."

Unbelievable, isn't it? We suspect that no meaningful interaction ever went on between Isaac and

Rebekah. Just mundane comments like, "What's for dinner?" or "What's the weather like outside?"

Here are some other examples of circular communication. Add some of your own.

_____ "My mother only speaks to me about her problem with my sister."

_____ "Everyone tells Mom their problems and lets her work them out."

_____ "I can't talk to my older sister; she just gets angry so I tell my other sister what I want my older sister to know."

_____ "Mom always talked to Dad for me."

_____ (Write any other examples of circular communication in your family of origin.) _____

_____

Family myths, family secrets, circular communication—families caught in these destructive cycles are also usually locked into rigid family roles, which serve to keep us stuck in dysfunctional patterns.

Family Roles

The more destructive the cycle of the family system, the more rigid the roles in the family will be. And these roles will help to perpetuate the dysfunction, just as the other destructive traditions do. Research on the family has identified at least seven different roles that are found in our families of origin and are often duplicated in our own families.

Two of the roles are assigned to the parents. One parent is usually the *problem*, and the other is assigned the role of *chief enabler* of the problem. This is most easily seen when one of the parents is alcoholic and the other parent keeps the problem in place. Sometimes the problem is workaholism or unfaithfulness or abuse or incest. Usually when one parent is the problem, the other parent somehow enables the continuation of the problem, even though he or she might protest and claim the opposite. The husband who moved his family every time his wife was admitted into the mental hospital was the chief enabler in that family.

Sometimes the problem is between the parents, as in the case of Jacob and Esau. It's hard to decide which parent was the real problem—probably it would have been Rebekah and her manipulations. But a more obvious problem existed in that there was no real relationship between the parents any longer. They both were the enablers of the problem in that they did nothing to confront it and change things.

Usually, one of the children takes the third role, what we call the *enabler-in-training,* or the one who helps the parental enabler do his or her job. Jacob would have been the enabler-in-training in his family, for he was following in his mother's footsteps (he was part of the plot to deceive his father and obtain Esau's birthright). Then he went on for graduate training under the direction of his mother's brother, Laban, who tricked Jacob into marrying his elder daughter, Leah, when Jacob had been promised the beautiful younger daughter, Rachel.

Sometimes the chief enabler gets tired or sick, and someone else needs to carry the problem for a while. In one particular family the husband was a severe alcoholic who frequently threw up and passed out. His wife would clean him up, put him in fresh pajamas, and put clean sheets on the bed. He'd wake up the next day and deny that anything had ever happened. She couldn't prove it because she had cleaned up all the evidence. She did this for years.

Then one night, the Dad passed out in their son's bathroom downstairs. The mom looked at him and gave up. Instead of cleaning him, she went upstairs to bed. But the son got up, cleaned up the mess, helped the dad up the stairs, and put him into bed. He did everything Mom had done for years, including washing his clothes. Yet, no one told him to do it; he just knew he had to fill in the gap. This son will probably marry someone just like Dad someday. And he will teach his children to be enablers-in-training so the destructive pattern will be passed on from generation to generation.

A fourth role that one of the children takes is that of *scapegoat,* the problem child in the family. This child often takes on the role of scapegoat out of loyalty to the family and in order to take the focus off the real problem, the parent. Esau was probably the scapegoat in his family, at least from the point of view of his mother. Nothing he did was of any value to her, he just went fishing and hunting most of the time.

Another role one of the children takes is that of the *family hero,* the child who makes the family look good to the rest of the world. To be a hero, you don't have to be a lawyer or a doctor, although that would really be great. The hero in one family, for instance, was the one son who held the same job for over eighteen years. He was the only one in the family who had been able to hold a steady job. His role as hero was to make the family look good to outsiders.

A sixth role often taken by one of the children is the *comic,* the person who adds humor to an otherwise bleak situation. When the tension starts to build because of problems, this person has something funny to say or do to make the rest of the family laugh. Comics often play this role everywhere in their lives, some even becoming professionals.

The seventh role is that of the *lost child,* the child who is on the fringe of the family. Often, a parent will unknowingly say of this child, "He just never was any trouble. You hardly knew he was there." This child never makes any waves. He or she is often like a lonely satellite revolving around the family, outside looking in.

We don't necessarily play these roles out in society, but we do play them out in our families. And when we start our own families, we usually pick up somewhere near where we left off. People look for relationships in which they can act out their roles. Family relationships are made up of people who, outside their homes (or otherwise in the absence of their partners), are perfectly capable of functioning satisfactorily and who, when interviewed individually, may appear very well-adjusted. This picture changes dramatically when they are seen together with their "complements"—family members who are needed in order for them to play out their role.

Which of your family members do you see in each of these roles? (If there are fewer than five children in your family, a lesser role is sometimes left out, such as the comic. Or it may be that someone takes on more than one role.)

Parents: Problem _____
        Chief Enabler _____
Children: Lost Child _____
        Hero _____
        Enabler-in-Training _____
        Comic _____
        Scapegoat _____

Family myths, family secrets, circular communication, and family roles—all these destructive patterns have a way of repeating themselves. That's why they are so frightening. If we don't learn from the past, we're bound to repeat it. The pattern goes from the parents' families of origin to the present, immediate family. We're not as free and independent to set up our own families as we'd like to think.

The Multigenerational Pattern

Psychologists call this repetition of destructive patterns the multigenerational pattern of abuse. In Isaac and Rebekah's time, they said it this way: The sins of the fathers will be passed down to the children and the children's children to the third and the fourth generations.[3]

The multigenerational pattern was as obvious a couple of thousand years ago as it is today. Remember when God told Abraham to leave his father's land and go to a new country? Abraham and Sarah then began wandering from place to place. Sarah was far from young at this time, yet she must have been quite a beautiful woman because Abraham was worried that the kings of those foreign lands might look at her and think, *What a beautiful woman! I want to marry her. So I'll have her husband killed so I can have her.*

So Abraham said to Sarah, "When we get to Egypt, we're going to tell a little lie. We're going to say you're my sister so they won't kill me."

Where was his faith? It wasn't so great at that moment. He was as human as you and I. His faith carried him in the long run, but he had lapses in the short run. If God was going to provide an heir through Abraham as He had promised—and hadn't yet—how could these people kill him? But Abraham didn't think about that.

And sure enough the king of Egypt, the pharaoh, fell in love with Sarah and took her into his harem. Soon some terrible things began happening to Pharaoh. We can imagine what he might have said when he finally confronted Abraham: "Hey, Abraham, everything was going well in Egypt until you came along. Could that be a coincidence? Or is there something more going on here?" When Abraham told Pharaoh the truth—that Sarah was his wife—Pharaoh sent both Abraham and Sarah on their way.

You'd think Abraham would have learned his lesson. But he did the exact same thing some years later with King Abimelech.[4]

Have you ever noticed that Isaac repeated the pattern? After the death of his father, Abraham, Isaac told the same lie to Abimelech, king of the Philistines—that his wife, Rebekah, was his sister.[5] As a young man, Isaac may have been bothered that his father had lied. He may have even determined that he would never do that. But he did.

There was another, bigger multigenerational pattern in this Old Testament family. Let's go down through the generations, beginning with the first generation, Abraham and Sarah.

Abraham and Sarah had two sons, Ishmael and Isaac. You may think Ishmael wasn't their son, but he was. Although Sarah's maidservant, Hagar, gave birth to Ishmael, Ishmael was considered to be Sarah's son because she owned Hagar. And he certainly was Abraham's son.

Sarah didn't want anything to do with Ishmael after he was born, however. Then along came Isaac. Sarah felt he was the perfect child, and she invested all her time in him.

When Sarah said, "I want Hagar out of here, and I want that kid Ishmael out of here too," Abraham gave Hagar a lot of money and sent her off. But he never dealt with the real issue, the favoritism that started with Abraham and Sarah over Isaac.

Isaac repeated this pattern, but just a little differently. He probably subconsciously said, "I will never play favorites as my father did." But when his wife, Rebekah, favored Jacob, he probably was reminded of his mother's overpowering connection to him. Subconsciously, he said, "I've got to do something to save Esau." So, again, we have favoritism being shown, only in a little different form because the mom and dad are divided over it. Each has a favorite. That's the second generation.

The multigenerational pattern continued into the third generation, to Jacob's family. Jacob added his own little twist to the pattern. He had favorites not only among his children but also between his two wives. Jacob, you will remember, was tricked on his wedding night by his manipulative uncle, Laban. Laban substituted Leah, his plain older daughter, for Rachel, the beautiful, younger sister whom he had promised to Jacob. Jacob got Rachel a week later but had to work seven more years to earn her hand. Leah, the older sister, was neglected by Jacob in comparison with the favor he showed Rachel. And Jacob's favoritism continued toward his children. He very obviously favored Rachel's two sons, Joseph and Benjamin, over Leah's sons.

The pattern of dissension between children went from Abraham to Isaac to Jacob and then continued through the history of Israel in the rivalry between the two tribes—Israel and Judah. These biblical families were similar to ours today.

Another part of this pattern is that in each generation, one of the sons was sent away. And each time, the circumstances surrounding his being sent away became more violent and dysfunctional. Ishmael was sent away because Sarah was angry. Jacob was sent away because Esau was angry and threatened to kill Jacob. Joseph was sent away, narrowly escaping with his life, as his brothers plotted his death, deciding only at the last minute to sell him into slavery.

Check the patterns below that have been repeated in your family throughout the generations.

_____ The habit of playing favorites
_____ Lying and dishonesty
_____ Alcohol or drug addiction
_____ Sexual addiction
_____ Verbal abuse (yelling or verbal put downs)
_____ Suicide
_____ Sexual abuse
_____ Write any other patterns you see in your famiy _____

Family myths, family secrets, circular communication, and family roles keep us stuck in multigenerational patterns of abuse. With all of these factors at work within a family system, which is doing all it can to resist change, you can see how powerful the family system is and why it is so hard to break free from these patterns. The result is usually the same: more of the same.

Summary

Can we break the traditions of our families, or are we destined only to repeat them? The answer is that we can unpack the baggage of the past and break free from the cycles that block us. But it takes hard work and courage. The roles we learned in our family need to be understood in order for us to overcome them. The myths, secrets, destructive communication patterns, and family roles have to be identified and brought into the open. The process begins with awareness, followed by understanding. As we begin to unpack this baggage from the past, we begin to break its power and its hold over us. But there's another piece of baggage we bring into our marriage, which we need to understand: the influence our parents have had on our ability to trust.

9

Our Parents' Impact on Our Ability to Trust and Be Trusted

ONE OF THE things Jan and I wished we had known when we got married was the importance of building trust. We didn't even expect that trust would be an issue—we just assumed it came along with our marriage vows. Our first apartment was in the home of an eighty-plus-year-old woman, Mrs. Tallman. She had built two apartments in her home to house married students, and we rented the one on the main floor.

It was a difficult arrangement, especially for newlyweds. The apartments were incomplete. They did not have separate bathrooms; we shared one with Mrs. Tallman and the upstairs apartment. Our apartment included the original kitchen of the house and one other room, which had the walls painted green and the ceiling painted blue. "Just like outside," she said. Since we had the kitchen and Mrs. Tallman didn't, she assumed she could use ours—at least our refrigerator. Even though it wasn't part of our rental agreement, she would put a few things in our refrigerator and come into our apartment whenever she needed those items. We don't have to describe how embarrassing that could be. It wasn't a very emotionally "safe" way for newlyweds to live.

Talking to Mrs. Tallman about our need for privacy did no good. We soon learned that we couldn't trust her to do as she said. We needed a boundary between us and her. We finally bought a new doorknob with a lock on it. When locked, the doorknob on her side would just spin. She never could figure out how we could make the doorknob work and she couldn't. Gradually she gave up and accepted the reality that she couldn't come in anymore and began using the small refrigerator she kept on her sun porch.

Our inability to trust this woman to understand what we needed in terms of privacy was similar to our struggle to learn to trust each other. For instance, I assumed that if I had to work late, Jan would understand. I didn't need to call her ahead of time to let her know. And when I decided to change jobs, I didn't talk to her about it; I just went ahead and did it. The more of these things that happened, the more difficult it was to build the kind of trust that fosters intimacy. And the more I did without consulting Jan, the more things Jan did to get even. She went out and got a job without even consulting me. "Just a little surprise," she said with a smirk on her face. This is how it goes when two people do not understand the importance of building trust.

Trust is the keystone to love. Experiences in our early childhood, as well as later experiences in our lives, often affect our ability to trust.

Foundation of Trust

How do we learn to trust? According to Erik Erikson, trust is the first major task of life. Some even say that it begins within the womb. Studies by David Spelt and others have shown that a fetus can learn a conditioned response to a noise and remember it for several weeks. Obviously, these memories are intimately connected to the mother. The fetus experiences the emotions, the stress and tension, as well as the joy and pleasure the mother is experiencing. If the mother does not want the child, or if she is anxious about the pregnancy, the fetus will experience these feelings, and this will affect the child's ability to trust or to feel wanted and safe after he or she is born. Therefore, the mother's role in the development of trust is primary. After all, she is usually the first one there. As a result, much of what we learn in the area of trust is built on what we experience with her.

The Mother's Role

Mothering is not an easy task today, what with all the books, articles, and classes that either tell a woman how to be a perfect mother or point out all the things she has done wrong. Fortunately, the ideal position is somewhere in the middle, being a "good-enough mother," but not a perfect one. Three destructive mothering styles—the hovering mother, the emotionally absent mother, and the uncertain mother —tend to hamper our ability to trust other people and, therefore, hamper our ability to build intimacy.

The Hovering Mother

Some mothers are "too good," in that they are constantly there, hovering in case the child needs something. We have talked with a number of mothers who were neglected by their own mothers and, in reaction to that neglect, have provided too much for their own children. They never allow their children to experience normal frustration.

Carrie was raised by this type of mother. As a little girl, Carrie could not escape from the presence of her mother. She did not have a problem with it when she was little, because she and her mom were always special to each other and they enjoyed each other. She was an only child, and her father deserted both of them when Carrie was about five. She and her mother clung to each other because they felt that neither one had anyone else to depend on.

We met Carrie as an adult, and as we talked together, she made it very clear that one of her main issues had to do with trust. She trusted no one, not even her mother. She went on to explain that her mother didn't seem real to her, since Carrie could do nothing wrong in her mother's eyes. But instinctively Carrie knew that she wasn't perfect. After some years of testing this premise by seeing how much she could get away with—staying out late at night, going with the wrong crowd, experimenting with alcohol and drugs—Carrie decided that her mother was just not honest about her response to Carrie and what she was doing; therefore, she was not trustworthy. She was "too good" of a mother. She had tried "too hard."

Carrie also had a related problem. She was experiencing terrible relationships with men, partly because she did not trust her own thoughts or feelings about them. She had never had to make a decision or express a need as she was growing up because her mother anticipated everything, even things she didn't really want or need. As a result, Carrie had no way of learning how to trust her own instincts about anything, but especially about her feelings toward other people.

As an adult, Carrie had difficulty maintaining any close relationships. She often found herself idealizing other people, and then when they could not live up to her idealized image, she would drop them. If a young man survived that test, competition would develop between him and her mother. The competition was not just her mother's doing. Much of it took place inside of Carrie, who wondered what her mother thought about this young man and whether or not he met with Mom's approval. Later in this chapter we'll see other ways Carrie's mother contributed to some of her relational fears of closeness.

The Emotionally Absent Mother

Chris's mother was just the opposite of Carrie's. Both his mother and father were alcoholics. His primary memories of early childhood were of waiting in the family car, all by himself, while both of his parents sat in the local bar getting drunk. His other memories included being left with baby-sitters or relatives who didn't really show any concern or interest in his needs. And when he was only seven, Chris was made the baby-sitter to his younger brother. Chris remembered feeling totally responsible for himself and his little brother the many long nights his mom and dad were out drinking. Chris took this job very seriously; he had been beaten by his drunken father several times because neither of the boys was asleep when their parents came home. Chris determined at a very early age that since no one was going to take care of him, he was on his own. Trust? Why should he? He'd take care of himself.

When Chris came to the clinic, he had run dry of any ability to take care of himself. He felt lonely, isolated, and cut off from his own family. He trusted no one, not even God. He'd been very active in his church, teaching classes and helping whenever needed, but his experience told him that when the chips were down, even God was nowhere to be found. He felt deserted by everyone. It took some time for him to see that trusting was the core issue for closeness and that he had no foundation for it from his early childhood. This made it impossible for him to trust anyone or even to understand what trust felt like.

Chris, like Carrie, expected idealistic relationships and was disillusioned when the other person was flawed in some way. But Chris had grown tired of trying to connect with other people and decided that the possibility of being close to another person was just a fantasy.

A third style of mothering is a combination of the "too-good" mother and the neglectful mother: the uncertain mother.

The Uncertain Mother

The kind of mother who is uncertain and unsure of herself is one who vacillates between the extremes of the "too-good" mother and the neglectful mother. Sometimes this mother is warm and nurturing; other times she is cold, busy, and rejecting. The child just doesn't know what to expect from her.

Marge, the woman mentioned earlier who was raised in a home in which her mother constantly criticized her father, had a mother who was uncertain. Most of the time her mom was warm and nurturing, but out of the blue she would severely criticize Marge or someone else in the family. When you met Marge in Chapter 2, she was doing the same thing to her husband that her mother had done to her. She and her husband were in a "come close/get away" kind of relationship as Marge had experienced as a child. But now Marge was perpetuating the cycle.

Marge desperately wanted to be close and to trust others, but she kept setting herself up to be hurt and criticized. And if that criticism didn't happen, she would push other persons away by criticizing them. She was caught in a vicious cycle because she had not yet faced the truth about the kind of relationship she had had with her mother and how that affected her in her present relationships.

Think about your own mother. Was she:

_____ A hovering mother?
_____ An emotionally absent mother?
_____ An uncertain mother?
_____ Other? _____

How about your spouse's mother? Was she:

_____ A hovering mother?
_____ An emotionally absent mother?
_____ An uncertain mother?
_____ Other? _____

The mother's role is primary, but the father's role is very important as well.

The Father's Role

Children need touch and care from their fathers as well as from their mothers. Touch is an important ingredient in the shaping of our ability to trust in later life. Touch allows us to form a bond with another person. An example of this is demonstrated in an experiment in which money was purposely left in a phone booth. The experimenter would approach, say the money was his, and ask for it back. The money was seldom returned to him unless the experimenter touched the other person. Touching made the experimenter more trustworthy. Then, very often, the money was returned.

Studies conducted in England after the second World War showed the importance of touch to the physical well-being of infants. The mortality rate in children's orphanages was very high. Exceptions were found, and invariably the reason was that someone was holding and touching the children on a regular basis.

Touch is also an essential ingredient in the emotional development of a child. Studies have shown that children who are not touched are more prone to violence and drug abuse. I've found that children who were not touched much by their family grow into adults who do not like to touch or be touched. Usually they have a difficult time trusting as well. Touch and nurturing are as important from the father as they are from the mother. It is critical that we receive this touch and care from both parents so we can learn to trust.

Yet a number of studies have shown how little the average father is involved with his children, especially when the children are at a young age. Many fathers are absent because of their work. Others are no longer a part of the family because of death or divorce. Often, fathers are not very trusting themselves, especially in the area of emotions, and are anxious about touching their children. Their anxiety can be felt by even the smallest baby (that is, assuming the father is even attempting to build a relationship with the child).

When the father is absent because of death or divorce, a stepfather often appears on the scene. The natural bonding that usually takes place in infancy is not there with the stepfather, so the child takes longer to learn trust. If the child is sexually molested by a stepparent, he or she will have even more difficulties trusting. The important boundaries of self have been violated in the most personal and sensitive areas of the child. This is true whether the perpetrator is a parent, a stepparent, or some other adult.

One of the primary roles played by the father is to provide an alternative nurturing figure so that the infant will not be overwhelmed by the mother as the one loving object.

The Father as an Alternative to Mother

Not only do we learn how to bond and attach to someone else in the first couple years of our lives, but we also need to learn how to be a separate and distinct person. We need to separate from our mothers. Take the child who is a year-and-a-half. He's just learning to say "No!" Or he's angry at his mother because she has done something he doesn't like: She has told him he couldn't play with that beautiful vase on the table, for instance. The child needs to have a father he can turn to when he's mad at Mother, because the father will help to contain the child's anger so that the mother isn't "destroyed."

The child has an omnipotent belief at this time of life. He mistakenly thinks, "If I get angry at Mom, I might destroy her. Then there won't be anyone there for me." If Mom's the only person there for him, he has to stuff all his aggressiveness and deny that it exists because he doesn't want to destroy, and therefore lose his mother.

When fathers are absent, either emotionally, physically, or both, children feel consumed by the mother, and then the problems experienced with their mothers will be intensified.

Like mothers, fathers also adopt destructive parenting roles—the absent father, the abusive father, and the strong, silent father—which will hinder the child's later ability to trust.

The Absent Father

Terry's father died when Terry was nine. Over the years, Terry had idealized his dad, so Terry really missed him. He felt a lot of emotion whenever he talked or even thought about his dad. His mother was so committed to taking care of Terry after her husband died that she never remarried, partly because she didn't feel she could take the time away from Terry. As he grew into his teens, he was her companion whenever she needed one. He became the "man" of the house.

Terry never had much of a chance to grieve for his father, since he had to be strong for his mother. All through high school and into college, he felt responsible for taking care of his mother, which took a lot of his time and energy. He didn't have much time or emotion left over for male or female friends either.

As a result, he didn't really know much about himself or what he wanted out of life. He fell into a relationship that led to marriage. He started a career path that was moderately satisfying. And he held back in every situation he was in for fear that he would lose whatever sense of self he had left. He felt insecure, lacked confidence, and ended up reacting to everything rather than taking responsibility for himself.

As we talked, Terry began to see that his father had been absent long before he died. Terry had several selected memories of his dad on which he had built his idealized image, but when he finally looked at his dad more realistically, he had to admit that his dad really had never been there, except for a few occasions Terry had treasured. His absent father had shaped his future relationships and relational abilities.

The Abusive Father

Ann had the opposite experience with her father. Ann's father was a very present raging alcoholic who could just as easily beat up one of the kids as take a breath. She had been raised in an environment of fear and abuse. She remembered her father beating her for the smallest infraction and her mother sobbing silently in the doorway.

Ann had a history of relationships with men who were just as abusive and explosive. As her own kids grew older she decided that the safest thing she could do was stay away from all men. But then she didn't trust women either, for they appeared weak and helpless to her. As her own daughter got into high school and developed friends her own age, Ann felt increasingly cut off from everyone, including her own children. When a parent is abusive, it is easy to see how the child will have difficulty learning to trust other people, even those who would appear to be easy to trust.

The Strong, Silent Father

The role the father plays is usually passed on to the sons. In our culture the "real" man is still seen as indifferent and silent. This "real" man is supposed to be like the Lone Ranger, who rides off in silence at the end of each episode, needing only the occasional conversation with his faithful Indian companion, Tonto. Intimacy in the lives of countless examples of other Western heroes and private detectives is the fleeting romance that is here for a moment and then gone.

The image that the strong, silent male is a reflection of deep and profound sensitivity is compounded by the impression often given in stories and fantasies. Even though this is true only in the mind of the viewer, the result to the child is the same: a lack of intimacy and closeness built on an inability to trust anyone. In recent years, this inexpressive type of male behavior has lessened in popularity, but it is still there within men, fighting against the real work of building intimacy. The macho father affects both sons and daughters and isn't much different from the absent father.

Think about your own father. Was he:

_____ An absent father?
_____ An abusive father?
_____ A strong silent father?
_____ Other? _____

How about your spouse's father? Was he:

_____ An absent father?
_____ An abusive father?
_____ A strong silent father?
_____ Other? _____

Your parents and your spouse's parents are like powerful shadows in your marriage.

That Old Cycle of Repetition

When our mothers and fathers do things that make it difficult for us to trust others, we usually seek relationships that somehow allow us to work out these original conflicts with our parents. Many times, people see the destructive pattern of their behavior, and because they do not know how to stop themselves, they simply end a relationship. Others find themselves caught up in a vicious cycle where they feel attracted only to someone who resembles the difficult parent. That old song "I Want a Gal Just Like the Gal that Married Dear Old Dad" has more truth in it than we might imagine, especially when the gal that married dear old Dad was and is still a problem to us. (Or when the guy that married dear old Mom is a problem.)

When we follow this pattern of looking to a present relationship to resolve a past conflict, we set ourselves up for failure. A woman told us recently that she married her mother in her first marriage, and then married her father in her second marriage. Both marriages were unsuccessful attempts to work through unfinished emotional issues with her parents. Her experience is quite common and only reinforces her own worst fears and compounds her problem. Those who do this now have additional reasons not to trust others and to protect themselves.

Roberta's dad was an alcoholic who left her mom when Roberta was in high school. As soon as she graduated, she married someone who also happened to drink a lot. Her brothers and sisters tried to warn her, but she was in love. At first, Roberta felt that Jack was still having fun with the guys and that when they had kids he would grow out of it. But the kids came along, and Jack drank even more. One night as she cleaned up the mess he had made when he got sick and then passed out, she realized that she had married her father. But she was determined she was going to make it work; her husband wouldn't leave her the way her dad had left her mother.

And for twenty-eight years Roberta was the perfect codependent for Jack's alcoholic behavior. She knew about his affairs but attributed them to the alcohol. One day he announced that he had fallen in love with the latest woman and would be moving out. She felt as if someone had cut her legs out from under her. That was five years ago, and she still has difficulty facing the reality that she is divorced. She can remember the pain of the marriage, but she feels happy that she has at least stayed married longer than her mom did.

Roberta is not interested in dating anyone, not only because she is afraid she will simply repeat the pattern but also because she feels she gave her marriage everything and that wasn't enough. She isn't about to open herself up to anyone else and fail again. She, like others who have been deeply hurt in relationships, has sealed herself off from being hurt again, choosing to trust no one.

Roberta is imprisoned by her fear of abandonment. Therefore, she can't trust. All of these parenting styles we have mentioned lead us to be overwhelmed by fear, particularly the fear of abandonment and the fear of being consumed.

Facing Our Fears

All of us have fears. It's a normal part of being human. But two basic fears are related to childhood issues with one or both of our parents: fear of abandonment and fear of being consumed. These two fears deeply affect our ability to trust.

The Fear of Abandonment

Children who grow up in a family in which the mother and/or father is either not there or is emotionally unpredictable and inconsistent will often experience feelings of abandonment. These children have a very critical attitude toward themselves, often blaming themselves for not having their needs met by their parents. They feel somehow at fault. This leads to feelings of insecurity and badness, and a sense that their needs are greedy, way out of proportion to what they should be.

As these children become adults, they sometimes give up on ever having their needs met by another person. Some of them choose to withdraw into a lonely, isolated world of their own, as Chris did, where no one is close enough to hurt or disappoint them. Some of them still have a private fantasy of what it would be like to be close to another person and to be nurtured, but they have given up hope of ever experiencing it in this life. A more common pattern, however, is for these adults to work very hard at doing everything right, for then they may earn the right to be cared for. They become perfectionistic, trying harder and harder to serve the needs of the other person in the relationship, believing that eventually the other person will take care of them. Usually, though, their fears of abandonment will take over and they will blame themselves when the other person does not show caring.

Marianne was afraid of being abandoned. Her boyfriend had been paying a lot of attention to her girlfriend, and when she confronted him about it, a huge fight resulted. She was angry, and she let him know it. But as soon as he left, her anger turned to panic. She had thoughts like, "I'm sure I was wrong. I just overreacted. Maybe he'll never talk to me again. I really blew it this time. I've got to get control of myself in these kinds of situations. It's all because I feel so insecure, just as he says."

She baked some of his favorite cookies and drove around looking for him so she could apologize for her terrible behavior. We asked her what she had done about his flirting with her girlfriend.

She had to think for a while before saying, "Oh, that. I guess it was my fault for not being understanding. I guess I just made too much of it."

The problem is nothing had changed. Her boyfriend's behavior would continue, and Marianne would keep blaming herself and apologizing in order to make peace. And everything would stay just the same because Marianne was so afraid of abandonment. Since the day her father had left home and hadn't come back, she couldn't tolerate any repetition of those abandonment feelings.

The younger you were as a child when an injury took place, the more blame you will put on yourself. Children are very ego-centered; they see themselves as the cause of everything that takes place in their world. If Marianne's dad left home when she was five or six, her natural tendency would be to think that she was somehow to blame. As a child, Marianne tried to be a better daughter, thinking that would make her daddy come home. As an adult, she was still trying to do everything perfectly, so that those she cared about would not leave her.

The Fear of Being Consumed

Carrie, the girl who grew up with the hovering mother, had the opposite fear. She felt that if she didn't get away from her mother, she would be consumed by her. Because Carrie had not worked through her feelings about her mom, she repeated that relationship with others in her life. Her last boyfriend complained that she was too independent and that she hadn't been that way at the beginning of the relationship. But at the beginning everything is so exciting and easy, especially for people like Carrie. It's what happens later that makes it difficult.

As her relationship continued for several months, Carrie felt more and more crowded. Her boyfriend needed too much from her. He wanted to spend every minute with her. He was too dependent, she thought. The only way Carrie could protect herself from feeling that she was going to be consumed by the relationship was to back off and distance herself from him.

Carrie often found herself getting angry at those who were close to her, particularly her boyfriends, for not understanding her need for personal space. She avoided her mother, who now lived two thousand miles away, by leaving her telephone answering machine on and calling back only when she felt her mother was really getting exasperated with her. But when someone asked about her mother, Carrie spoke about her in glowing terms. "We're really there for each other. She's the most important person in my life probably." She hadn't been able to separate herself emotionally from her mother in a healthy way, so she was still fighting the feeling of being consumed by anyone who cared for her.

When we asked Carrie whether she felt that she would be consumed by her mother if she weren't careful, she thought for a moment and then said, "Yeah, that's exactly how it feels. I guess that's why I moved halfway across the country from her when I finished college." Until Carrie got her mother into a proper perspective, she would always fight against closeness in all her relationships while at the same time seeking it.

The Push-Pull of These Two Fears

Of course, these two fears don't operate in isolation. We will experience both of them. Often, our fear of abandonment causes us to try very hard in a relationship, and when we suddenly find that we are closer than we care to be and feel engulfed, we back off from the other person in an effort to regain some comfortable personal space. But then the fear of abandonment rises up within us again, and we start to move back toward the other person. When you add the fears of the other person to the equation, you can see why closeness and intimacy take a lot of work and require a foundation of trust.

We often are attracted to people who are trying to work through the opposite fear from ours. Those who most fear abandonment like to relate to those who most fear being consumed. On a rational level that doesn't make sense, but fear causes us to operate on the irrational level most of the time.

(A lot of marriages represent the push-pull of these competing fears. One fear dominates in one person and the other fear dominates in the other person.) Breaking this cycle is not as easy as it looks. For one thing, if I fear abandonment, I will do a lot of things for the other person in order to keep him or her interested in me and liking me. Since I am such a good caretaker, the other person has it made—or so it seems. That person doesn't need to do much to keep the relationship going—just be sure not to stray too far away. But this little system we have set up fails to take into consideration that other person's probable fear is that of being consumed.

In our culture the woman usually struggles with the fear of abandonment and the man struggles with the fear of being consumed. But we've met couples who are the opposite and the problems we will describe are the same.

One way of understanding this is to look at a marriage relationship as a set of two circles within a closed economy. Many people, when they are in the beginning stages of a relationship, think the two circles should look like this:

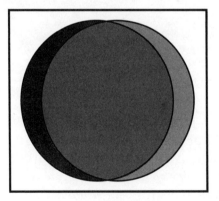

But that's too much closeness for the person with the fear of being consumed. There is no guarantee that the person who emerges from that kind of symbiotic, fused relationship will be me; it could be you. So after the first fight, the two circles may look like this:

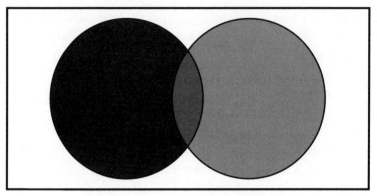

After a series of exchanges, the relationship may settle into a pattern that looks something like this:

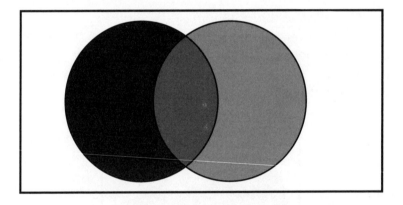

Now let's put some symbols into the diagram to help us understand the push-pull that we often find in our marriages. We'll put a *T* in the overlapping parts of the circles for *togetherness* and an *S* in separate parts of the circles for *separateness*.

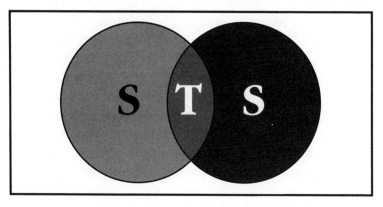

Then, we'll put a box around the circles to represent the family unit as a closed system, or closed economy. Let's suppose that in this economy there are two hundred coins. One hundred of these coins have a *T* stamped on them and represent the amount of energy that can be expended on *togetherness*. One hundred of these coins have an *S* stamped on them and represent the amount of energy that can be expended on the development of the *separateness*.

After a few years of marriage, the distribution of the coins will probably end up looking something like this:

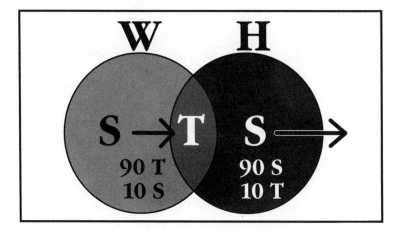

You can see the direction the energy will flow. You'll have a very stable, but unsatisfying, situation with one person spending the majority of her energy on building togetherness while the other person is directing his energy outside the marriage to develop *separateness* through his job, friends, or hobbies. One becomes the pursuer, and the other, the pursued.

Here the wife, fearing abandoned, places a lot of her energy and effort into working on the togetherness in their marriage. She expects them to spend time alone together on the weekends and encourages her husband to leave the office at 5:30, rather than working late. The husband, fearing that he will be consumed, puts a lot of effort into doing things independently, acting very responsibly in his job and hobbies "for the sake of the marriage." He's likely to say, "I work sixty to seventy hours a week for my family." The wife, who feels abandoned, doesn't see it that way.

What needs to take place for this relationship to be more satisfying for each person? Unfortunately, the burden of the work falls on the one who is already doing most of the work. But a different kind of work is required. In fact, the person who has the most togetherness coins is going to have to give up some of them. This means she is going to have to stop being so responsible for nurturing the relationship, to stop being the pursuer.

It's important how the pursuer handles this change. Often some changes occur when the pursuer gets totally fed up and reacts with cold, hard anger. But when this happens, the person with most of the *separateness* coins puts some down and picks up a few of the *togetherness* coins until the pursuer cools down and things can get back to normal.

Megan tried to reverse the roles in her marriage

during a session in our office. At first we thought she was really going to change her pattern of pursuit. She reacted with quick, hot anger to something her husband, Steve, had just said. As she grabbed a pillow and threw it at him, she announced, "I've had it! I'm through with this marriage!" And then she just sat there and glared at him. He had a silly, embarrassed smile on his face at first, but when she stayed mad, he started to squirm.

"I'm sorry," he began. "I know what I just said was stupid. I can't believe I said it. You're not going to end the marriage over that, are you?"

His question went unanswered.

I didn't want to jump in yet because I wanted to see where Steve, the typical workaholic, would take it. His family was one of the symbols of success he had gathered around himself. Now, it was in jeopardy.

Steve went on for at least twenty minutes, going from apology to promise as he pursued Megan in order to try to win her back. She started to smile, but kept the angry glare in her eyes focused on Steve so that he wouldn't get off the hook. At the end of the session, they were talking together and had made plans to go out to eat in order to keep talking.

The next week, Megan said that Steve really tried for several days, but now they were right back where they had started. When Megan's fears of abandonment had subsided, she had unconsciously gotten back into her role of being responsible for their togetherness. Her fear of abandonment returned, and Steve got back into his role of seeking separateness. It had only been a temporary reversal of the cycle; nothing had really changed.

In order for there to be a real change in the way they related, Megan needed to back off on some of the things she did to keep them together and put more energy into her own life. But she needed to do this graciously and without hostility in order for it to be effective. And she needed to keep on doing it, even after Steve began to work on their togetherness.

For example, after the session in which Megan angrily stated that she was finished with the marriage and Steve began to make some moves toward her, she needed to let go of the anger, but hold on to her resolve to begin to take better care of herself. She could have said to Steve, "I know what I said was in anger, and I apologize for being so angry. I know I've been on your case for a long time. Part of the problem is that you have your work and your friends there, and I only have you and the kids to look after. I know I need to do something about that."

Megan did do something about it after our next session, and Steve didn't quite know how to respond. Now, the ball was in Steve's court. She found a class that she wanted to take and signed up for it. She made arrangements for a sitter so Steve could work as late as he wanted, and kindly told Steve of her plans. Now, Steve was even more confused. Megan made sure that she wasn't cold or angry, but she also made sure that she didn't chase after Steve, either. It wasn't easy, for these changes stirred up a lot of Megan's fears of abandonment.

After several weeks of this, Steve started to get anxious. He tried to pick fights with her, but she stayed in her cordial, but firm, position and refused to enter the battle. Next, Steve started coming home from work earlier, suggesting that they could use the time to do some things together. He started to act more insecure, and he became aware of some of his own neediness. Gradually, they began to work together on a more balanced relationship, as shown below. For both

Steve and Megan to maintain this balance, they would need to redefine their boundaries as a couple.

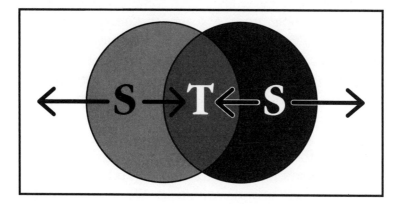

Defining Our Boundaries

Many marital conflicts are power struggles over the definition of the individual boundaries within the marriage. Boundaries are necessary. My skin is a physical boundary that keeps what is inside of me separate from what is on the outside. (It's the ability to keep Mrs. Tallman outside of our apartment!)

In marriage, personal and emotional boundaries are always issues that need to be resolved. Who I am, who you are, and who we are together are all boundary issues. When a person's boundaries are too rigid, they keep other people out. They are probably more afraid of being consumed than of being abandoned. These people feel distant toward other people, and other people see them as hard to get to know. In a marriage, they spend a lot of time working on the separateness issues.

On the other hand, people who have fuzzy boundaries often overidentify with their spouses or friends.

The wife finds her identity in her husband; the husband finds his identity in his work or his friends or sports and other activities. Each has fuzzy boundaries.

These people are easy to get to know, sometimes too easy to get to know. Other people may feel these people are too dependent; in the marriage relationship these people will often work very hard on togetherness issues. They have a hard time saying no because of their fear of rejection.

In order to develop our own personal boundaries, we need to work through our fears of abandonment and our fears of being consumed, and the reasons these fears are at work within us. When Megan tried to define the boundaries in their marriage, they were too close for Steve; he was afraid his own personal boundaries would be lost. When Steve tried to define the boundaries, they were too distant for Megan; she was afraid he would slip away from her.

Think about your own life. Your sense of personal boundaries is based on your success in building a solid, emotionally bonded relationship with your mother, and then being able to find some separateness from her through your relationship with your father. When this process is incomplete, you will experience problems with personal boundaries. You will have weak personal boundaries if you have not been able to trust both of your parents.

Are you afraid of abandonment? Or of being consumed? People whose fathers or mothers left home (or died) when they were young, or who were neglected because their parents were absorbed by an addiction, such as alcoholism or workaholism, for instance, often fear abandonment. On the other hand, people whose parents were the overwhelming, hovering kind often fear engulfment.

I fear:
_____ abandonment.
_____ being consumed.

Your fear is invading the way you interact with your spouse. If you are angry with your spouse because he or she doesn't spend enough time with you, your relationship with one of your parents could possibly be fueling that anger and making it much worse than it otherwise might be. That reaction could be causing you to be overly dependent upon your mate, which then causes him or her to run further away from you.

Or if you are constantly moving away from closeness and intimacy, it could be because you were consumed as a child. This can be very frustrating to a spouse, by the way.

Now think about your spouse. Does he or she seem to fear abandonment or being consumed?

My spouse seems to fear:
_____ abandonment.
_____ being consumed.

Finally, how are the coins distributed in your family? Who holds the most *togetherness* coins (probably the one who fears abandonment, as Megan did)?

The one who holds the most togetherness coins in our marriage is: _____.

Who holds the most *separateness* coins (probably the one who fears being consumed, as Steve did)?

The one who holds the most separateness coins in our marriage is: _____.

How uneven is that distribution? Is it ninety to ten, as in the case of Megan and Steve? Or only sixty to forty, which is fairly even?

Write down your estimate of the distribution in

your marriage in the circles below (see page 191 for the earlier example of the distribution of coins):

_____ Husband

_____ Wife

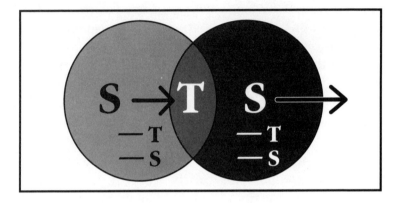

Working through our issues with our parents in a way that leads to forgiveness and release is an essential step in establishing healthy boundaries in a marriage. We suggest that our patients consider a five-step process.[1]

Forgiving Your Parents

1. Recognize the Injury

Begin by thinking about your mom. Was she a hovering mother, an emotionally absent mother, an uncertain mother? If she was, you have been hurt by your relationship with her, and you have experienced losses in your development. You need to work through these issues and ultimately forgive her before you can fully trust your spouse. Think about your childhood and describe one incident in which you felt hurt by your mom below:

Now think about your dad. Was he an absent father, an abusive father, or a strong, silent father? If he was, you have been hurt by your relationship with your dad, and you have experienced losses in your development. Think about one incident in your childhood in which you felt hurt by your dad and describe it below:

2. Identify the Emotions Involved

Think about that incident with your mom. Identify the feelings below that are closest to your own and complete the statements:
"I am afraid to look at this because _____."
"I feel guilty about _____."
"I feel ashamed and humiliated by _____."
"I am angry that _____."

Now think about that incident with your dad. Identify the feelings below that are closest to your own and complete the statements:
"I am afraid to look at this because _____."
"I feel guilty about _____."
"I feel ashamed and humiliated by _____."
"I am angry that _____."

3. Express Your Hurt and Anger

We treat this as a separate step because it is so important. It is not enough to simply identify what we are feeling. We also need some way to express our feelings. Imagine that Mom or Dad or both are sitting in the room with you. Tell them how you are feeling. (It is usually unnecessary for you to literally do this with either parent!)

If I could say anything I wanted to say to Mom, I would tell her, "Mom, you hurt me by: _____ _____."

"And I am angry about: _____ _____."

If I could say anything I wanted to Dad, I would tell him, "Dad, you hurt me by: _____ _____."

"And I am angry about: _____. _____."

4. Set Boundaries to Protect Yourself

As we mentioned earlier, a personal boundary is what defines who I am, apart from you. Our boundaries can be too rigid or too fuzzy. Ideally they should be flexible, yet firm.

Think about what you can do if your parents are alive, to set new boundaries with Mom. (For instance, "I will not allow my mother to make me feel guilty about not following her advice." Or "I will not call her every day as she would like me to. I will try to be my own person.") Set two new boundaries in the spaces below:

1. _____.
2. _____.

Now, think about what you can do to set new

boundaries with your dad. (For instance, "I will not allow my dad to control me by shouting at me.")

1. _____.
2. _____.

You may want to talk to someone you trust about what you have written before moving on to the final step.

5. Cancel the Debt

Once you have worked through the first four steps you are ready to forgive. This involves releasing your parents (or parent) from your own expectations. Cancel the debt they owe you. You do this to set yourself free. Often it helps to make the act of forgiveness take some concrete, tangible form. You may want to write *forgiven* over your description of the incident in Step 1.

Once you have done this work within yourself effectively, you can be in the presence of your parents and feel, on the inside, that you are the age you are. If you still feel, on the inside, like a kid or an adolescent, you still need to do some work in these areas. It takes two grown-ups to experience an intimate marriage.

Summary

We've been looking at some of the barriers we encounter in our search for closeness. We've seen how our family-of-origin issues, our fears, and our personalities can set up roadblocks for us as we seek intimacy. Once we understand these hindrances, we can begin to take some positive steps in order to build a more loving relationship.

We need first to understand that intimacy is not a

goal in and of itself. It is much like happiness: the more you actively seek it, the more elusive it becomes. Intimacy is a by-product of the right kinds of behaviors. If we use these behavioral building blocks, we will experience closeness and intimacy. In the last section of this book, we will identify these important building blocks.

PART FOUR

The Building Blocks of a Loving Relationship

10

Caregiving

SOME YEARS AGO we participated in a marriage conference in which Charlie and Martha Shedd were the banquet speakers. We were fascinated as they talked about their marriage and the things they did to keep the fun and the mystery in their relationship. One of the things they told about struck both of us. They said that whoever brushed his teeth first in the morning put toothpaste on the other person's toothbrush! A small thing, but a sign of caring.

The next morning, one of us, I don't remember which one, after brushing his or her teeth put toothpaste on the other person's toothbrush. We hadn't talked about it, but we both had the same idea. For years now we have not missed a morning doing this simple little act of caring. Even when things are tense between us, that tension is sometimes broken by a toothbrush that already has toothpaste on it. And never, in all these years, has either one of us felt like we "had to do it." It was our *gift* to the other.

The first building block in the development of a healthy relationship is the concept of *caregiving*. Most people say, "That's easy. I care." But we must make some careful distinctions here in order to understand what we mean by the term *caregiving*.

Caregiving vs. Caretaking

When we talk about caregiving it is important to distinguish it from caretaking. Most of us care about the other person. However, something happens to that caring when it is expressed, and most of us end up being caretakers. Caretakers take over for others. They make the decisions. They control other people's behavior. They dominate. Sometimes they hide behind such statements as "I'm only doing this for your good."

By contrast, caregivers offer help. They're there when needed, but only as much as they are needed. "I won't do for you what you can do for yourself" is what a caregiver says. Caregivers accept responsibility for their own actions, but refuse to cover up or take responsibility for the decisions or actions of others. Whereas a caretaker takes responsibility for the other person, the caregiver simply "gives care."

Many of our relationships get tangled up in caretaking. When there isn't enough love, openness, trust, and honesty in a relationship, people become caretakers. They can't express their needs openly or directly, so they go underground, thinking that if they take care of someone, somehow it will come back to them.

In order to further understand the difference, we will contrast the seven negative characteristics of caretaking with the positive characteristics of caregiving. As we do so, analyze your relationship with your spouse. Are you a caretaker or a caregiver?

1. Caretakers Expect a Payoff

Maggie literally bubbled as she talked about helping her new neighbors. The husband was still over-

seas with his company, and would be there for another three months. The wife and two children settled
in, but in adjusting to living back in the States, the
children had one kind of sickness after another.
Whenever they needed anyone or anything, Maggie
was there—baby-sitting, running errands, or filling in
so the mother could have a little time to herself. When
the new neighbors started to attend church with Maggie, she was almost ecstatic. When the husband finally rejoined his family, they all attended Maggie's
church together. They came a couple of times, but
then they stopped coming.

Maggie was devastated. She bitterly complained to
another friend, "They're going to another church. Can
you imagine that, and after all I did for them!" Up
until that point, we could have said that Maggie had
been a caregiver. Now, if we had to categorize her,
we'd say that she had made herself into a caretaker.

The difference rests in motive and expectation.

Suppose Maggie had said, "Well, they decided on
another church, but we're still great friends. We really
have a good time together." That kind of response
would be what a caregiver might say. It would reflect
an unconditional giving of herself to her new neighbors.

There is no question that Maggie was kind, caring,
and helpful. But she had set up expectations in exchange for her help. Even though she never verbally
said, "I'm helping you so that you will be so grateful
you will become a close friend and even attend the
same church I do," her response to their actions made
it clear that this was part of her expectation.

That's how caretakers operate; they often have subconscious motives and expectations that go beyond
caring.

2. Caretakers Control

The popular word today is *control.* Yet we are really talking about power. It's a show of force, a way to dominate.

I remember talking to a mother who did everything for her four children, even making their underwear! "It's my way to show them how much I love them," she said when people commented on her self-giving. But that was only one side of the woman. Until the day she died, she expected a phone call from each of her children *every day.* If they made decisions without consulting her, she felt rejected and pouted for days.

Several years ago, one of her sons accepted a job promotion that required him to move to a town about six hundred miles away. His mother called him every day, making him feel guilty and disloyal for "leaving the family." Within a year, this son quit his job and returned to his hometown. He found another job that wasn't as good and didn't pay as much as the one he left, but at least he was near "home." As people watched this mother relate to her adult children, it was obvious that she exercised control over them. She had all the power.

The opposite of power is helplessness. Some people become caretakers because they are afraid of their own helplessness. They think of themselves as strong personalities. They concentrate on taking care of the weak, those they think are not able to do for themselves. As long as they give, do, and serve, they don't have to think about themselves and their own feelings of helplessness.

3. Caretakers Set Conditions and Demand That They Be Fulfilled

One afternoon, as I was driving somewhere, I was flipping through the dial on my car radio. I picked up a station that played the "golden oldies." The disc jockey was introducing a song sung by Doris Day, saying, "Ah, here's a beautiful and tender love ballad."

I don't recall all the words, but the music was soft and romantic as Doris Day asked something like, "Will you be true? Will you be kind?" She asked a number of other questions in the song, all related to how a man might treat a woman. When she got to the chorus, she urged the man to think it over and if he could say yes, then her final words were, "Then I'll give my heart to you." It sounded more like a contract than a loving commitment.

Whoever wrote that song wanted a caretaker, not a lover or a caregiver.

Relationships with caretakers often end up feeling like a business arrangement. The terms of the contract may not be spelled out very clearly, but on some level the caretaker and the one taken care of each know her or his part of the arrangement.

I remember one of my professors lecturing on marriage. One of his major points was that most couples operate on the principle of a *quid pro quo*. That's a Latin legal phrase that means "something for something." His premise was that marriages work on the idea of balance. If the husband gets to buy something, then so does the wife. If she buys something foolish, then he gets to do the same thing. It's a way of keeping score. It's really a way to set conditions, to give in order to get—and if the rules are broken, watch out!

4. Caretakers Manipulate

When we think of the word *manipulation,* most of us think of the demanding, sneaky boss who makes us feel guilty if we don't work twelve hours a day or the salesman who makes us feel guilty for not buying a product. Guilt is one of the most common methods used in manipulating others.

Manipulators do not have to be as bold and obvious as the salesman; they work quietly as well. Often it's the soft voice that says, "I work so hard to make this a beautiful home for you to relax in, and you want to go out for the evening?" Or "I spent a lot of money on your birthday present. I thought you'd at least try to keep the house cleaner." Whether loud or soft, the caretaker is able to make the other person do what he or she wants.

5. Caretakers Are Codependent

Codependents are individuals who give, often lavishly, but do it at the expense of their own needs, and with the expectation of getting something in return.

These are the people who give and give, never taking days off, hardly knowing what a vacation is, and. they would do more if they had more hours. Doctors, lawyers, social workers, ministers, therapists, and many others in the "helping" professions are all prone to being codependent caretakers.

These people are often rewarded for their efforts by words of appreciation or tears of gratitude, which often make them ready to throw themselves into the midst of caring again.

But try the other side. What if they are not appreciated? Not recognized? Not valued? Often they get thrown off balance and feel confused. Sometimes they get depressed and may even feel suicidal. They are trying to earn acceptance by caring, and when they don't get their wages they feel rejection.

Caretakers often gather stories about those who selflessly gave of themselves. Their favorite is probably the story of the Good Samaritan, who found the half-dead traveler on the road and cared enough to get him to some help. They never see that the caring person knew how to set some limits in this story. He did what was needed and then went on with his own business.

Too much of any good thing is too much. When people give and give and give with some conscious or subconscious expectation of getting something in return, they are fit candidates for codependency and caretaking.

6. Caretakers Carry Responsibility for Everyone and Everything

Those who really get caught in the trap of caretaking become responsible for everyone and everything.

* "Our marriage would be better if only I. . . ."
* "My children would do better in school if only I. . . ."
* "My parents would be happier with each other if only I. . . ."

Of course, the subtle trap in each of these statements is that often we really don't have that kind of control over a situation, and when we can't improve it, we feel guilty and inadequate. That guilt only serves to urge us to try harder, as Wendy, the mother of two preschool children, did. She told us, "I got so caught up in being responsible for everyone I began to see myself as the center of the universe, trying to hold everything together."

Wendy didn't realize what she was doing until one summer afternoon when she planned a picnic for the family. Her husband took the day off, and all of them headed to the beach. Just as they were starting to enjoy themselves, dark clouds streaked across the sky. Wendy said, "I watched them, thinking that I should have planned the picnic for yesterday, which was a beautiful day. I thought, *It's all my fault that our day is going to be ruined.*"

Of course, we all know that none of us can be responsible for the weather. But when we think as Wendy did, we are not thinking rationally. We are responding emotionally as caretakers for other people.

As Wendy's mind played over and over, she suddenly realized that she had made herself responsible for everything, especially everything that went wrong. That day was a turning point for her. She told her family, "We'll just eat early and wait for the rain to blow over." Since she stopped being responsible for the whole world, her relationships with her husband and her children started to improve. She was moving toward caregiving.

7. Caretakers Speak with Many Voices

Caretakers say one thing and never pay attention to the meaning behind what they are saying. For example:

- "This is what you should do."
  (Meaning: "I know what's best for you.")
- "Honey, don't be so sharp with the boy. And, Ron, you listen to your father."

(Meaning: "I know how to fix your relational problems.")

- "You don't need to be afraid of the dark. There's no one in your room."

(Meaning: "You don't need to feel what you feel, so I'm helping you to realize that.")

Caretakers have good intentions, but they don't understand the motives or hidden messages that accompany their caring. The problem is that the object of their caring often does hear the covert messages, and instead of drawing the two closer together, caretaking pushes the other person away.

If I try to control your responses or tell you what you will need to do to earn my caring, then I'm not moving toward intimacy. Remember, our definition of *intimacy* is "the joyful union that comes from loving and being loved." Anything that stops the flow of that love, such as bartering for my love, hinders intimacy.

Now, let's contrast these seven destructive characteristics of caretaking with the five positive characteristics of caregiving.

Caregiving

Just as caretaking adds barriers to intimacy, caregiving provides important building blocks for greater intimacy. Marty finally discovered the difference. One thing people who knew Marty agreed on was that he was one of the most generous men they knew. But that wasn't enough for Marty.

He understood the difference some months after joining a men's group at his church. The group was discussing giving. Marty said, "Something about needy people draws me. I want to do everything I can for them. But lately I've realized that nobody gives to me. Is it because people don't think I have any needs? I'm doing all the giving. Why?"

"Have you ever let anyone give to you?" asked another man in the group. Marty started to answer yes, then he thought a moment and realized that he hadn't.

The other man said, "You're a model of a generous person, Marty, but I don't really know you. I think you hide behind your generosity, and that gives the appearance of a person who doesn't need anybody else."

As Marty talked with the group about his reaction to what he'd been told, they promised that they would start giving to Marty. When he told me about the incident, he didn't use the word *intimacy*, but he said, "You know, I'm almost sixty years old. I finally feel like somebody really knows me. I love those guys because they hung in there with me when I didn't know what I was doing."

That's a good description of intimacy.

Intimacy means that we stop being caretakers and learn how to talk openly about things that are important to us. When we take a risk by letting others know where we stand on issues that mean a lot to us, we're also opening the door to intimacy. We realize that we can be who we are in relationship to others *and* allow them to be who they are. Marty valued the men in his group because "Nobody told me what I had to do to get better, or how fast I had to do it. They just said, 'Marty, we're here for you if you need us.' " This is caregiving.

1. Caregiving Expects No Payoff or Reward

That's the obvious side of what we've just said. Yet one of the hardest lessons we have to learn is that intimacy grows out of an acceptance of who we are, and it is not based on what we do or don't do. We often understand this concept intellectually, but it seldom penetrates to the depth of who we are. Instead we subconsciously believe in the following equation:

My caring + your responding in the way I expect you to = intimacy.

When we become caregivers, the formula looks more like this:

My caring + 0 = my part of building intimacy.

Obviously, my caring alone cannot create intimacy; that's why we work so hard on the other person's response and end up being caretakers. But caregiving gives love and caring with no expectation of reward. It's unconditional.

You can see how this can tap into our fears and our old family patterns. Our immediate fear is that if we love the other person unconditionally, he or she will abandon us or take us for granted. Our fears cause us to pull back and set some "reasonable" conditions, but the result is always a lessening of intimacy.

Immediately, your thought may be, "But that's a set-up for someone to take advantage of me." That's a risk, but that's also the risk of finding intimacy.

2. Caregiving Allows Others to Feel for Themselves

Those who seek intimacy don't want to see the ones they love hurt, but caregivers don't try to clear the roads, sweeping away everything to prevent any possibility of suffering. Caregivers allow suffering, pain, heartache, and rejection. They know they can't really stop others from feeling the hurts of life. What they do know is that they can be there with love and support when the one they love hurts.

Margie was trying to become a caregiver, rather than a caretaker. She told us about her response when her husband came home, crushed because the promotion he had been counting on and working so hard for had been given to someone else.

As he stood by the sink, telling her of his hurt and disappointment, it was all she could do to keep herself from jumping in with suggestions of what he should or shouldn't do. Her husband just kept talking as she stood silently next to him. When he finally paused, she put her arms around him and with tears said, "I'm so sorry." Just that. They held each other tight for several minutes, and then he started talking again.

That night as they lay in bed, Margie's husband said to her, "You know, I don't know what's happening to you, but I feel like you really understood what I was feeling. That was special." He went on talking, telling her about some of his fears and concerns about not getting the promotion. She said to me, "For years I've been trying to get him to talk like that to me. I guess all I needed to do was shut up and show him how much I really care."

3. Caregivers Know That They Are Needy

Maybe this is obvious, but we think that many of us still hold to the misguided idea that it's selfish to have needs.

Many of our churches have added to our mother's

admonitions and examples that truly caring people have no needs, no desires, and no feelings about themselves. What we have failed to understand is that when we lose touch with our own needs, our hearts can fill up with self-criticism, self-blame, and self-doubt.

We all are needy people. If our needs go unmet, or if we don't acknowledge them, we're left unfulfilled and discontent. That's the reason we become caretakers. If we cannot express our own neediness, we have to do nice things for others with the hope that they will do something in exchange for us. Caregivers think in terms of caring for others *and* taking care of their own needs. This means they have learned how to tell someone what they need.

4. Caregivers Face Their Own Vulnerability

If caregivers know they need love, understanding, friendship, intimacy—and acknowledge those needs —they will find themselves feeling quite vulnerable. "I need . . ." and "I want . . ." are vulnerable statements. To some, just thinking of their needs can be terrifying because it places them in the precarious position of being rejected and/or abandoned.

When a wife says to her husband, "I need you to just hold me," she is giving him power over her. He can comply, but he can also react by walking away or saying something like, "I'm too busy right now" or "Later." That's the kind of rejection she's desperately trying to avoid.

We've already looked at the importance of trust. To be vulnerable means we are learning to trust the other person with ourselves. As that trust builds we develop a sense that the other person won't take advantage of us, or knowingly hurt or abandon us.

Caregivers are saying, in effect, "I want to be cherished for who I am without manipulating you or pretending I don't have needs." They are also saying, "I trust you enough that I'm willing to put myself in the place where you can reject and hurt me."

That really is risky! That's not easy to do, but it is a necessary step in building intimacy and closeness. Rather than shield our vulnerability from others and close off the possibility of creating and maintaining intimacy, we open ourselves to the other person. Often, vulnerability is seen as weakness. The truth is that it takes a special kind of inner strength to assert our genuine feelings.

5. Caregivers Are Aware of the Power Issues

As we've seen earlier, all couples struggle over the matter of boundaries within the relationship, and it is always a matter of control. Intimacy requires us to come to terms with how we influence or affect the behavior of the other person.

Most of the power issues in a relationship have to do with the setting of boundaries within that relationship. A boundary defines where I stop and where you start. Boundaries also define who I am in the relationship and who you are in the relationship. This includes what each of us does in the relationship.

Caretakers ignore boundaries. They take care of everything, even when the person could do it for himself, or when they don't want another person to do it. Caregivers allow the other person to be who he or she is. They don't intrude or try to control things that are the responsibility of the other person. That's why the caregiver allows the other person to feel what he or she feels and to take responsibility for her or his own life.

Stop a moment now to evaluate your own relationships. Are you a caretaker or a caregiver? Check the statements below that apply to you:

_____ I expect to receive some payoff when I help someone else.

_____ I want to control the relationship.

_____ I tend to keep score. I have an unwritten set of conditions for that relationship, and I tend to demand some payment.

_____ I might use guilt to manipulate others.

_____ I tend to be codependent.

_____ I carry responsibility for everyone and everything.

_____ I don't tend to expect a payoff.

_____ I allow others to feel for themselves.

_____ I know I am a needy person.

_____ I face my own vulnerability.

_____ I am aware of the power issues in a relationship.

If you checked any of the first six statements, you have some caretaking tendencies. If you checked most of the last five statements (or all of them!), you are a caregiver.

Now think about your spouse. Check the statements below that apply to him or her:

_____ My spouse expects to receive some payoff when he or she helps me or someone else.

_____ My spouse wants to control our relationship.

_____ My spouse tends to keep score. He or she has an unwritten set of conditions for our relationship, and he or she tends to demand some payment.

_____ My spouse might use guilt to manipulate me or someone else.

_____ My spouse tends to be codependent.

_____ My spouse carries responsibility for everyone and everything.

_____ My spouse doesn't tend to expect a payoff.

_____ My spouse allows others to feel for themselves.

_____ My spouse knows he or she is a needy person.

_____ My spouse faces his or her own vulnerability.

_____ My spouse is aware of the power issues in a relationship.

If you checked any of the first six statements, your spouse has some caretaking tendencies. If you checked most of the last five statements (or all of them!), your spouse is a caregiver.

If either you or your spouse tends to be a caretaker, there is always an opportunity to change. If you work through the issues discussed in Parts Two and Three —your fears of abandonment or engulfment and the issues related to your experiences in your family of origin—you should be able to make the transition from caretaker to caregiver. Caregiving behaviors and attitudes may stir up these old issues, but caregiving is one of the essential ingredients in building intimate relationships with those we love. It's worth the effort and the risk.

Caregiving List

As a couple, you may want to make a list for the other person of some simple, concrete, positive things your spouse could do *for you* to show you he or she cares, like putting the toothpaste on your toothbrush. You might put on your list something like: "Call me from the office and ask me about my day"; "Make my favorite dessert for me"; or "Fill my car with gas without telling me."

The more items you can put on your list, the more things your spouse can do to show you that he or she cares. Often, the things we put on our list are some of the things our mates did for us when we were courting. That's part of the reason those days felt so special: We were doing small, concrete, pleasing things for the other person. And we cared enough to find out what was pleasing to that person, rather than do what we thought was pleasing.

Try to think of at least ten things. Write them down and then give your list to your spouse. Your mate will also give his or her list to you. Do at least one thing from your spouse's list each day. You don't have to do everything on your mate's list. It's your choice. Do this for thirty days and see what a difference it makes.

But remember, this is a list of things that are meaningful to you, not a list of things your spouse is required to do. You and your spouse can only be caregivers if there is no obligation or expectation of return. Then you are each giving a gift of love.

11

Forgiveness

TIM CAME HOME from work, and the living room looked as if it hadn't been swept. (It hadn't.) The children seemed to have left almost every toy they had on the floor all through the house. (They had.) He turned to Verna and said, "You know how upset I get when you let the living room get messy. Can't you ever keep it clean? You are the messiest housekeeper in this town!"

His words shocked Verna. Instead of screaming back at him, she said quietly, "This is probably only the third or fourth time this has happened in the five years we've been married. Come on, now. My not cleaning up the living room isn't what's bothering you. Something else is."

"I just can't stand your messes!" Tim yelled as he stomped out to the backyard.

Sometimes hurtful things are done in a marriage, which gradually, or suddenly, erode the foundation of intimacy. Hurt has been added to hurt over the years by the continued failure of the couple to work out a problem, or some form of betrayal has instantly destroyed what it has taken years to build. Tim was close to destroying the foundation of their relationship.

Before Verna reacted, she reminded herself that forgiveness was going to be her goal. She was learning that forgiveness was a process and that, as with any process, *it begins with a decision*. She chose not to react to Tim's outburst.

Forgiveness Begins with a Decision

(Forgiveness is an act of the will, something we choose to do because we know it is healthy and right, even though we may not "feel like it" at the moment.)

We have increasingly come to believe that we don't really have any choice when it comes to forgiveness. Too many important things are said in the Bible about the necessity of forgiveness. For example, in the Lord's Prayer, Jesus tells us to say as we pray, "And forgive us our debts, As we forgive our debtors." He goes on to say, "If you forgive men their trespasses, your heavenly Father will also forgive you. But if you do not forgive men their trespasses, neither will your Father forgive your trespasses."[1] Paul picks up Jesus' urgency when he tells us, "Be kind to one another, tenderhearted, forgiving one another, just as God in Christ also forgave you."[2]

Frank Minirth and Paul Meier, the cofounders of the Minirth-Meier Clinics, are well-known for their belief that a great deal of life involves our choices. "Happiness is a choice," they said in their book about depression. "Love is a choice," they said almost ten years later in their book about codependency. We'd like to add another choice to that list: "Forgiveness is a choice." Verna had to choose to *want* to forgive her husband for accusing her of being "the messiest housekeeper in the town." She made the decision to forgive, but the final part of that choice—the forgiving —was still out there in the future.

(The decision to forgive is the first step in the process of forgiving.) But the whole forgiveness process usually gets stymied before it's begun because certain barriers keep us from moving forward.

Barriers to Forgiveness

The Myth "Forgiving Is Forgetting"

One barrier to forgiveness is the myth that *if we have forgiven, we have forgotten.* This is impossible. It is important for us to remember what we are forgiving so we can learn from our experience. If Verna tries to forget her husband's unfair accusation in order to forgive him, she may be setting herself up for him to say the same thing again. God can forget when He forgives (as it says in Isaiah 43:25) because He has no need to learn anything from what happened.

Forgiveness is defined as *cancellation of a debt.* We may cancel the debt, but we still know the debt existed. Verna does need to let go of the emotional debt she feels her husband owes her. But that doesn't mean she must forget what he said. In her case, a debt may be owed to her, but usually there is no way to collect it. It can only be forgiven.

(We can forgive whatever hurt we have experienced, even though we cannot forget. It may take time, for as David Augsberger has said, "Forgiveness is a journey of many steps." But husbands and wives will forgive if they are willing to admit their own human failures and, drawing on their own experience of God's grace, extend grace to each other. Once you've chosen to forgive, the road involves a lot of hard work, resolving the feelings of hurt within, as well as the anger at the betrayal.) A second barrier to forgiveness is our problem with anger.

Anger

It's not wrong to experience anger. God placed the emotion of anger within us for a purpose. It is a way to stand up for ourselves and protect our boundaries.

It sends a strong message of "No" to the listener. We may be powerless to change the situation, but expressing our anger at an injustice enables us to acknowledge our frustration and make a statement. When expressed in a proper way, it can be a doorway to greater intimacy, rather than a barrier. For anger to become this doorway, we need to take four important steps.

1. Anger Needs to Be Acknowledged and Understood

Healing in a broken relationship has to start with a self-examination that is brutally honest.

It's often much easier to be honest about what *we think the other person has or hasn't done,* but seldom does that kind of honesty lead anywhere positive or constructive. We need to begin the healing process by becoming honest *with ourselves about ourselves* and about what we are feeling—especially about our anger. In effect we are saying, "I am responsible for who I am, for the choices I've made, for the consequences of my choices, and for the feelings I have."

Tim needed to think about Verna's response to his accusation—"My not cleaning up the living room isn't what's bothering you"—and admit that something lay behind his present anger, which was causing him to be unreasonable. Confession to ourselves about our failures is an admission that we have done things we know were harmful to ourselves and to our relationships. Most of us don't like this kind of honesty, but the restoration of intimacy in strained relationships always begins here.

If I'm angry, I need to be aware of that fact, as well as be aware of what I am angry about. That may sound elementary, but too many of us are angry and either deny the fact that we are angry or blame someone else for our anger and refuse to take responsibility for what we are feeling.

For example, Jim came into the clinic because he was struggling with his anger. He said he had yelled at his wife, Beverly, because she said something about wanting to take the kids to Disneyland that summer. "All you ever want to do," Jim shouted, "is spend my hard-earned money. You don't understand how hard I work to provide for this family!"

Jim needed to stop and look at his anger. He wasn't in denial about being angry, but he may have been in denial about what he was really angry about. Perhaps his anger was at himself for feelings of inadequacy or worthlessness, which really started to hound him when he found out his best friend was taking his family on a five-week vacation. Perhaps Jim was angry because he felt insecure about his job, due to a "not-so-good" review by his boss a couple of days earlier. If Jim could identify what he was really angry about, his anger could become a doorway to greater intimacy rather than a barrier.

2. We Need to Talk About What Is Really Going On

Both Jim and Beverly needed to understand what was really going on, so it was important for Jim to talk to her about his anger.

After Jim cooled down from his tantrum, he needed to sit down with Beverly and discuss what he thought he might really be angry about, instead of simply throwing out an embarrassed "I'm sorry" to her. As they talked together, their understanding of each other's behavior and attitudes deepened.

Or think about Tim, the man who told his wife, "You are the messiest housekeeper in town." As Tim cooled down, he started to explore what he was feeling about the day. Finally, he had to admit to himself that her leaving the living room a mess reminded him of the everyday situation in his home when he was growing up.

His mother was a terrible housekeeper, and she never seemed concerned about it. She always had some other project going on, such as her gardening, crafts, or other activities. The house wasn't that important to her. It wasn't that it was dirty; there were just messes and piles of things everywhere. Tim was always too embarrassed to have friends over.

When Tim yelled at Verna, he was displacing his anger. He was yelling at her when he was really angry at his mother. We all do this to some extent. A father is speeding, and a police officer stops him and gives him a ticket. His daughter says, "Daddy, you did a bad thing." He yells at her. He isn't really angry at her; he's angry at his own behavior, and he needs to acknowledge that fact.

A couple we know have a saying they repeat to each other whenever anger comes out. Each of them says, "I'm seldom angry about what I think I'm angry about." That's all. But it helps them pause and examine what's really troubling them. And because they can do that they are able to talk together about what's going on inside each of them. Maybe that's part of the reason why they seem to have a deeper sense of intimacy with each other than other couples we know.

3. We Must Want to Understand the Other Person

Beverly could easily respond to Jim's anger with her own anger. She could have shouted back, "I didn't ask you to take me to Disneyland, I just thought you might like to be a real father and take your kids there."

As she gets her dig in, Jim escalates the argument with something like, "Oh, yeah! All you ever want to do is spend money." And on and on it would go with new hurts and injuries added with each exchange of words.

If Beverly has internally made a decision to try to understand why Jim is angry, she will be able to work through her hurt to the point where she can begin to forgive him as they talk about his anger. Beverly can break the cycle of hurtful anger and set up a foundation for forgiveness and greater levels of intimacy. The key to forgiveness in a marriage is the desire to understand the other person. Sometimes it helps to take the other person's point of view for a moment, or even to switch roles in the argument. As you start to make the other person's point, you will often realize how he or she is feeling.

4. We Need to Respond to the Deeper Level of Understanding We Have Developed

In this case, Beverly can respond to Jim's feelings of inadequacy (the bank account was dangerously low at that time) or his anxiety (over that "not-too-good" review). When we respond to the deeper levels, looking at what might be behind the anger, we make it safer for each one to be more open within the relationship.

Sometimes, though, we cannot really identify the reasons for our own hurtful behavior. We've worked with a number of couples where one party has had an affair. Often the spouse fixates on finding out why the affair occurred, as Bryan did with Jill. The betrayed spouse sets out to gather all the facts he or she can find, only to realize that the reasons for this hurtful behavior remain elusive.

In each case where this has happened, the search for understanding has become the mission of the injured party. When this happens, communication shuts down, and efforts to restore the relationship are blocked. At some point the affair needs to be set aside in the discussion. The more a spouse learns about the details, the more needs to be forgotten, and the more difficult it is to forgive. Understanding may not always be related to "Why?" Usually, it takes a professional counselor to help the individuals affected by an affair sort out all the deeper issues surrounding the hurt and betrayal that have been experienced.

The process of forgiveness can also take varying amounts of time, depending on the hurt or the injury.

The Time Needed to Truly Forgive

Some of us have been taught that *forgiveness is not genuine unless it is offered immediately.* While it is true that we are expected to begin to forgive quickly, the process of forgiveness often takes time. If we try to shortcut the required time for forgiveness, we end up not forgiving, but simply excusing the other person's behavior.

One couple we know has a simple little thing they do that helps them remember that forgiveness requires time and that healthy relationships require forgiveness. When one of them does something that hurts the other, they talk it through, and then the one who created the hurt says to the other, "What time will the forgiveness come?" The other one looks at the clock and, depending on the severity of the issue, suggests a time. Usually, one or the other remembers at that time and comments on the forgiveness. The injured party can say, "Yes, I can forgive you now," or "No, I need more time."

Some forgiveness, however, can be quicker, almost instantaneous, once we understand. Let's say that Jan is talking on the telephone and I'm not aware of it. I come into the house and turn the stereo up so the music "fills the place." Jan yells in frustration, "Turn that thing down!"

Her words are angry because she thinks I am being thoughtless, or simply because she has an important phone conversation. I can react in anger to her anger, as many of us do. But I could also quickly realize *my error* and not only turn down the music, but forgive her harsh words and ask her to forgive my thoughtlessness as well. Many of us who have been working on our relationships know enough about the other person that our understanding kicks in when a small disagreement like this occurs. Call it grace or love or all of the above—it sure helps in building intimacy.

But when we are dealing with the more severe kinds of problems that interfere with our search for intimacy, the hurt is on a much deeper level, and it will not be easy or quick to forgive. Some hurts are obviously big (like adultery), while others may seem small but are, because of a variety of factors, big to the persons involved (like Tim's aversion to a messy house).

Let's look at a situation that feels big to the person involved, but may not seem so important to others.

Hurts That Are Bigger Than They Seem

Randy and Lynn were married relatively late: Randy was thirty-two and Lynn was four years older. That never bothered Randy. As a matter of fact, he was very comfortable with it. "I never dated girls younger than me," he said. "I don't know why; I just didn't."

Randy wasn't the kind of husband who would say a lot of affectionate words, but he really loved Lynn. He did try to express his emotions by teasing—something he always did with his male buddies. As they shared some of this background, Randy told of a time he was talking with several of his friends and Lynn was standing by. He said, "Hey, you know something? Lynn was starting college when I was going into the ninth grade. I like having a woman of advanced age in my life!"

Lynn explained how that had hurt her. "It makes me feel like some dowdy woman who is old enough to be his mother." For years, Lynn had been trying to explain this to Randy, but Randy's response was always to make a joke of it.

Not long after our conversation, Randy and Lynn celebrated their tenth anniversary with some friends at a restaurant. Randy made a joking reference to his "old lady," and Lynn burst into tears and left the table. Randy jumped up to follow her as the others sat there, somewhat embarrassed.

Randy told us what had happened. "After a few minutes, we returned to the table. I said, 'You're all our good friends, so I don't mind telling you that I acted like a jerk. Lynn's been trying to tell me for years that I hurt her when I joke about her age. I want to apologize, both to her and to you all.' "

Lynn went on to explain that both her sisters were married young and had their families before they were thirty. They never said anything to her, but she always felt like the old maid of the family, the one that everyone feels sorry for. "So when Randy teases me, I know he doesn't mean to hurt me, but it hurts nonetheless." What might have been a small issue to someone else was a big issue to Lynn because of the things she attached to it.

Major Hurts

Probably the biggest hurt for couples is when one betrays the other. Having an affair with someone else is probably the most obvious and blatant form of betrayal. We've found that when handled properly, even the betrayal of an affair can be worked through, eventually forgiven, and the marriage relationship restored.

When trust has been broken by the unfaithfulness of one person, it is important to see that both people were usually involved in the creation of an environment that led to the affair. This does not mean that both people are responsible for the affair; only one person is responsible for making that choice. But both set up the kind of relationship that allowed this intrusion in their marriage. We've heard both spouses in this situation say, "I don't want to go back to the kind of relationship we had before the affair; it's going to be better!" And it can be better. In counseling, the focus needs to eventually shift from the affair to what needs to be repaired within the relationship, so that the couple can rebuild trust and intimacy.

Affairs are not the only form of betrayal. Disloyalty of any kind can be betrayal. John and Janet were a good example. John was a highly successful lawyer who was well-liked by everyone. But whenever Janet was in a group and John wasn't present, she seemed to find a way to talk about him. "He's an excellent lawyer, but he's a klutz around the house." Or "He can argue before a jury, but let a salesman grab him, and he's a sucker for every pitch that comes along."

It was not important that any of these things were true. It was a matter of loyalty to John. No one asked, "Is John handy around the house?" Janet simply volunteered the negative information about him.

She told us about the conversation that changed her behavior. She was with a friend named Shirley who was commenting on how nice Janet's house looked.

"No credit to John," Janet replied. "He just drops things anywhere and never picks up after himself. I suppose your husband does the same thing," Janet said to Shirley.

Shirley had listened to Janet's complaints a number of times. So she answered Janet by saying, "You'll never know, will you? If my husband has any faults, he'll have to tell you himself."

"I—I didn't mean to talk about faults," Janet stammered and half-apologized. Then they dropped the subject.

About a week later, Janet told us she called Shirley and told her, "Thanks for what you said. I've worked so hard on being honest, I didn't even realize that I was being unkind and disloyal to John."

Betrayal comes in many different forms. Given our human vulnerabilities, we probably have all experienced betrayal in some way. It always makes trust difficult, but sometimes we can get stuck in the process of forgiving and rebuilding that trust.

We remember talking with a man who had been an outstanding missionary in East Africa. He had gone to Africa soon after World War II and, because he had such a keen ear, he was able to pick up one dialect within four months. Over the first ten years he mastered four other tribal languages.

As we talked, I said something about the other people he worked with.

"I work alone," he said to me.

Something in the tone of his voice as he said that caught my curiosity. "Don't you have other friends who work with you at times?" I asked.

He shook his head. "I had a friend once," he said. "Once," I responded. "What happened?"

"He betrayed me. He talked about me behind my back."

I felt a great sadness for that man. He had never been able to trust again because he had been betrayed. Though I felt he was wrong in not forgiving, I could understand his pain.

He had become stuck in the process of forgiveness. He did not see the two sides to this process. We not only release others from their debt to us when we forgive, but we also find release for ourselves. In time virtually all the bitterness and hurt can be released. The missionary would still have a mental recollection of what happened (he had been betrayed by someone he trusted), and he would still be aware of the negative consequences that resulted from what his friend did. But what happened between them would no longer be a "live issue" in the way he thought of this person nor in the way he lived his life.

The important concept of grace makes the injunction to forgive possible. We know that we have been forgiven even though we have done nothing to deserve it. Because of God's grace, and forgiveness, we can forgive others. We are called to be forgiving people, especially with those we love. Unfortunately, that's where forgiveness is always the most difficult.

Look at why this is true. Two people have taken risks in moving toward each other. Gradually, over time, they open up parts of their lives to the other person so they can see inside. As they do, they develop a growing trust that leads to more freedom and openness.

Then one day, one spouse betrays the other in some way. The other is left hurt, alone, shocked, feeling used and abandoned. He or she quickly closes up the areas that have previously been opened. The other spouse may or may not be aware of what he has done. If not, this person starts to feel the same sense of betrayal in response to the other's distancing and begins to close up. Alienation, blaming, and other hurtful things may follow, setting up a deadly cycle.

Gary and Gale are an example of how this can happen in seemingly innocent ways. When they came to see me, Gary was angry because Gale had withdrawn from the marriage and was investing all of her time either at the church or at the high school their kids attended. "I don't think I even have a wife anymore," he said.

Gale described a marriage that had been going downhill for years. Gary was not one to share much about himself, and over time, Gale felt he had "frozen her out."

As they talked to each other in my office—the first time they had honestly opened up for at least five years—they both started talking about some very personal things that had hurt them in the marriage.

As the session ended, I asked them whether they wanted to save their marriage. They both sat there a while, and then Gary finally said, "If we could experience again what we've just experienced—this openness—maybe we could save it. But I don't know," his voice trailing off at the end. "Maybe we need to come here together and explore what we really want, before we decide."

After a number of sessions, they both decided they wanted to salvage their marriage and to be (in Gary's words) "a real couple." They did save their marriage, but it took a lot of work and a lot of forgiving. It also took a lot of time to repair the damage to trust that was done by the various ways they had betrayed each other over the years.

Betrayal can be complex. In Gary's case, his feelings of betrayal went beyond Gale's actual behavior. He told me that his parents had divorced when he was in junior high school. Both of his parents had had several affairs before ending their marriage. Gary was afraid that Gale's next step in withdrawing from him was to have an affair. She hadn't, but he was sure it was inevitable.

So part of Gary's work was to grieve over the betrayal he felt from both of his parents. His way of dealing with it had been to choke off his emotions and steel himself for the inevitable. He was on his way to being a cynical, bitter, betrayed man. But his grieving over what had happened with his parents, as well as over what was happening with Gale, allowed him access to his emotional side. He found healing within, which led to a restoration of trust between him and Gale. As they worked through the process of forgiving, they both were able to process their hurts and to rebuild a sense of trust between them.

We've seen how caregiving and forgiveness are two building blocks essential to building intimacy. Now let's look at the third building block, mutuality, which involves the give-and-take necessary for an intimate relationship.

12

The Give-and-Take of Mutuality

BRUCE'S FIRST WIFE died more than four years ago. For the past two years, he has been dating Cathy. They really love each other and have been talking about marriage, but Bruce keeps holding back. When we asked him what some of his fears were, he said, "I finally feel like an autonomous person. I think Cathy is also. That's one of the things I really like about her. So how do Cathy and I become intimate and still retain our autonomy?"

The words *intimacy* and *autonomy* have become buzz words, and for many people they seem contradictory. For Bruce, autonomy meant keeping his own life separate from his wife's. He loved Cathy, but he was not willing to surrender his life totally to her. Intimacy, to him, carried the sense of two people flowing together with their commitments, desires, and pleasures moving along the same track. He wanted to find personal fulfillment with Cathy, along with satisfaction in life. But if he were to give himself totally to another human, he feared that would keep him from being a person in his own right. In his first marriage, his wife kept pushing him for more togetherness. "It was as if she wanted us to escape from the world and merge into each other. She didn't say that, but I some-times felt she didn't think of me and of her as two people, only of *us*."

Bruce was trying to understand *mutuality* in the marriage relationship, which includes both intimacy and autonomy. But Bruce was hung up, like many of us, on his fear of losing autonomy.

We suggested that Bruce rethink his understanding of the word *intimacy*. We pointed out some of the things we've talked about in this book, that intimacy has to do with loving and being loved, of giving and receiving. It means closeness, but it doesn't mean get-ting rid of our own personalities to achieve that status. And intimacy has nothing to do with the fusion of one personality into another.

Erik Erikson, in his classic book *Childhood and So-ciety,* defined the eight developmental stages of hu-mans. He described the transition between adoles-cence and young adulthood as the crisis of intimacy. The way he defined *intimacy* included the idea of having the capacity to commit to specific affiliations and partnerships, along with the ability to develop the ethical strength to stay with those commitments, even if they call for significant sacrifices and compromises on our part. Intimacy is built on our successfully working through the issues of identity, which in-volves our ability to define ourselves as autonomous persons.

He also pointed out that if we had not had a good degree of success in the earlier transitional crises, par-ticularly the crisis of trust and of autonomy, we would have difficulty resolving the crises that come at later ages—namely, those of identity and intimacy. In other words, if we have not had trusting relationships and found the ability to define ourselves as autonomous persons in those relationships, we will not have the ability to experience intimacy (which is why we looked at how our past affects our relationships in Part Three of this book).

In his effort to understand mutuality, Bruce was raising the same question that many of Erikson's critics raised when they said that in his idea of intimacy, he was demanding a *selfless* devotion to the other person, a total giving away of the self. Autonomy would become lost in true intimacy.

What Bruce needed to see was that, first of all, intimacy involves commitment. Second, those in an intimate relationship grow and develop ethically and morally. Third, they stay with those self-chosen obligations, regardless of the cost.

We talked with Bruce about his earlier marriage and how those experiences probably blinded him to the true idea of intimacy. We went on to point out that intimacy is a commitment to another person, yet to sustain it, there is no question that it demands compromise. That's another way of explaining what Erikson meant by sacrifice. Rather than a loss of self, such a commitment requires an expansion of the self. An ability to identify with someone else's needs and feelings requires knowing ourselves.

We explained this to Bruce, and then added, "If you don't like words like *sacrifice* and *compromise,* think of it this way. Intimacy means being willing to be *inconvenienced* when necessary to satisfy those mutual feelings and needs within the relationship."

Bruce seemed to understand. "I'll have to give this some thought," he said.

When we consider mutuality and autonomy within intimacy, it seems clear that stretching ourselves in self-surrender does not mean we *lose* ourselves or that we fuse into another person. It does mean that we maintain an ongoing awareness of the other person's needs, and this requires an ongoing awareness of who I am. When both people are working at this together, intimacy *is* going to be the result.

"Intimacy speaks to me of my giving myself to my husband," said one woman, "and that kind of giving is without embarrassment, hesitation, or apology. Because I trust him, I know he won't make me try to become some other kind of person. He loves *me*. He wants me to be the best me I can be."

As we look at the give-and-take of marriage, the mutuality of two people, a number of things need to be a part of the relationship. This list does not guarantee closeness, but when both people are aware of these six components of mutuality, and incorporate them into their relationship, they will find a greater closeness.

Mutuality Requires Taking Off Our Masks

(One of the "sacrifices" that intimacy requires is that we take off our masks—those public images we hide behind—which are our own personally developed safeguards against being hurt. These masks keep us from exposing our innermost selves to other individuals. One of the hardest things for us to do is to get close enough to someone to allow that person to see the parts of ourselves that we've worked so hard to hide.)

I remember when I was taking a course in group therapy during my doctoral program. I volunteered for all of the groups because I really wanted to experience this type of therapy. I was sitting in one of the groups as the semester was winding down, thinking, *I really haven't done much in this group.* I recall thinking how some people in that group were intimidating to me.

Finally one day I said to myself, *Today I am going to take the risk and share something with the group.* As I did, I felt a tremendous affirmation from each person. It felt good.

As I was driving home, I thought, *Wow, that was incredible!* I started thinking about what would happen if I did the same thing with Jan. *Oh, yeah,* I remember thinking, *that could start some real problems.* But then I said, *No, I'm going to do it and see what happens.*

When I got home, I hemmed and hawed around for a little bit, and then I finally sat down and said, "I want to talk to you about something." I told her what had happened at group, and then I shared something with Jan that I'd never told anybody, one of the parts of me that I hid behind a mask. My hands were sweaty, and my heart was pounding a little.

Jan's response was to affirm me and then to share something about herself, something that was behind one of her masks. There was trusting self-disclosure by both of us and an empathic response as we mutually took off a mask and let the other person see something personal and scary about ourselves.

Mutuality Requires Us to Take Risks— Sometimes Enormous Risks

When Jan and I opened up to each other, we made ourselves defenseless. Because of our vulnerability, we could have easily crushed the other person with anger or laughter. Yet when we risked taking off those masks, we experienced a wonderful intimacy. (Finding intimacy *is* risky, even in a good marriage. One reason is that deep inside each of us lies a gnawing doubt about ourselves, about whether our mate would still love us if we told him or her about that part of ourselves. We don't open up because we're afraid to risk their disappointment or disillusionment with us. But when we do take that risk, the results are exciting.)

Mutuality Requires a Growing Acceptance of Each Other

When we looked at our personalities, we talked about the importance of accepting each other as we are. The point here is that this is a growing acceptance. Our mutual experiences with each other lead to the growth not only of acceptance, but also of trust.

I remember the experience of a husband who sat beside his wife's hospital bed. She had been in an automobile accident, and the doctors were not sure she would live. As he sat by her bed, in the middle of the night and the darkness of his fears of losing her, he let down all his defenses. Haltingly, and interrupting himself with tears, he poured out his heart, not knowing whether she could even hear him.

The wife did recover. Later she told him, "When I lay there, half-dead, I couldn't speak, but I could hear. Your words gave me so much hope. When you finally let me know how much I really meant to you, I begged God to let me come back to you."

The husband was surprised by his wife's acceptance of him and his feelings. It was the beginning of a deepening of their intimacy. He was ready to be more open because he knew she was ready to accept anything he might bring to her. It was hard work for him, but the rewards were great.

Mutuality Requires Time

This part of intimacy doesn't come easily, and it doesn't come quickly. It's built carefully, slowly, on block after block of trust, forgiveness, and acceptance. Time is its major element.

Mutuality is like planting a seed in the ground. For a time, everything takes place within the darkness of the soil. Eventually it breaks into the light, and then growth continues in both areas, in the emerging plant as well as in the hidden roots.

By its nature, mutuality is not stable. Just like a plant—which grows underground, sprouts, blossoms, and fades, only to start the cycle over again—the work of a relationship shifts back and forth between the two people. That's the idea of "give-and-take." Sometimes, one person will be overcommitted, leaving that person with little time or energy for the relationship, and the other person picks up the slack. When one needs to take more, the other gives more, knowing that over time the process will shift.

In some relationships this could feel like being taken for granted. In an intimate relationship, mutuality allows for these times, because each spouse shares a special kind of security with the other. *She's reliable,* he says to himself. *I can depend on him,* she affirms. These statements are based on a shared history, not just on what is happening in the present.

Sometimes both are overcommitted, and the work of the relationship is put on hold. Mutuality allows for these seasons as well. Mutuality knows the old lesson: "Sunshine without any rain only creates a desert." Dark periods are shared as well.

Suffering can be one of those dark periods. When one suffers, the other stands by that person, knowing that over time these shared experiences build a mutual history that is unique and special. True love is deepened when suffering is faced. Knowing each other's "story" adds to the experience of intimacy.

When we look back over the thirty-five plus years we've been together, we have often said, "If we can make it, anyone can."

Someone described marriage as an ocean, with its waves and troughs. We've had the waves, and we've enjoyed riding on the crest of them. But we've also had the troughs—deep ones, like financial troubles and difficulties with troubled children—just as you've had or may have.

In the darker times, we were sometimes so much at odds with each other, we felt things couldn't get worse. But our commitment to work together, not against each other, forced us to work through many of the issues we've described in this book. As we did, we found that in our pain, we drew closer to each other. When you make the choice to use even the painful times as opportunities to draw closer together, you will build a greater level of trust and intimacy into your marriage.

Mutuality Involves Exclusivity

Most people have several friends with whom they are able to share different things. One woman, who was a member of an Overeaters Anonymous group, told me, "There are things I tell the other people in my group that I just wouldn't tell any other friend." But she would not describe these friendships as intimate.

On the other hand, she spoke of her husband as her "best friend." By that she meant a special relationship, a togetherness that excluded others from its core. Each of them had opened the door to the core of themselves wide enough so that the other felt as if he or she had access. "It's like being entrusted with secrets that no one else knows," her husband added. "It feels good because I know she trusts me with things about her that she would never share with any other person in the entire world."

An intimate marriage depends, in many ways, on how special each partner feels to the other. We each need to know that we are the most important person in the world to the other person. When this is communicated and understood, intimacy grows and deepens.

Mutuality Requires Finding the Balance of Power

We were sitting at dinner recently with three other couples. All of us had been married at least twenty years. One couple, Lucy and Joe, had just celebrated their thirty-sixth anniversary. We decided to ask them about intimacy and mutuality. As we talked, the subject of power also came up.

"What's wrong with depending on someone else? What's that got to do with power?" asked Lucy.

"Isn't that giving him or her power in your life?" asked Norman, who had gone through a difficult time in dealing with his alcoholic parents and the effects of growing up in that atmosphere.

We all talked about it. Lucy summed it up by saying, "I guess we each have some power in the other person's life, but neither of us will abuse it. I know that no matter how tough the rest of my life is, Joe's always there for me."

Norman gripped his wife's hand as he said, "She

was there for me. I did depend on her. Some days I hurt so much I didn't think I could face any more pain. She never complained; she was just there. I don't think I could have made it without her."

We thought of Bruce and how he confused dependency with losing himself in a relationship. In true intimacy that just doesn't happen. No matter how close spouses are to each other, each of them is still a unique individual. As we looked around the table, that was obvious.

In several of the marriages both spouses worked outside the home. We call these "egalitarian marriages." But even that expression of individuality didn't take away from their relationship. They still saw themselves as "not free," and they wouldn't want to be. Each partner maintained an awareness of the needs of the other, along with the other's expectations.

Sue said, "Marriage sometimes puts limits on my independence, but it also expands who I am as a human being. After all, we grow by giving and by looking beyond our own needs."

As we all continued to talk, Lucy spoke up again. "I love Joe with all my heart," she said, "but I don't depend on him for my identity. I'm his wife. But remember, he's also my husband. And we're both still individuals."

"I'd say that Lucy doesn't need me to feel worthwhile," Joe added. "I'm good for her morale, and I tell her how important she is to me. But she's still her own person."

"I know who I am," Lucy continued, "and so does Joe. Isn't that part of what intimacy and mutuality are all about?"

"Okay," I replied, "but what if Lucy died. Could you live alone, Joe?"

They talked about that, and we all joined in. None of us liked the idea of one person's dying before the other, but the consensus seemed to be that probably one would die and the other would still be here. "That'll be tough, but we'll survive. And why not? We're still who *we* are."

The issue of power seemed to underline everything we talked about, but only indirectly, because the power issues had been worked out and there was a comfortable flow of power within each of these couples. They had found a balance of power in their relationships together.

As we watched the couples around our table, we noticed how much each of them enjoyed the other. They liked being together. Intimate people like being physically close. It's more than sexual; it includes touching, with both the hands and the heart. But then, when mutuality is present, they can also handle being apart.

One of the couples had totally different attitudes about travel. She loves to travel; he's burned out on travel, having been on the road for over twenty years in his job. She travels regularly with a group from her church, and he enjoys her enjoyment of her trips. His idea of a vacation is to rent a cottage on a lake and spend three weeks there. She spends part of the time with him, and enjoys his enjoyment of solitude the rest of the time.

Mortar Between the Bricks

The concept of mutuality is like the mortar between the building blocks of a marriage, which helps them fit together. There is a natural ebb and flow within the relationship that involves both parties. Both husband

and wife learn how to be caregivers, not just the wife. Both work at conflict resolution. When one can't, the other does. When one won't, the other will. That's mutuality.

An intimate marriage is filled with challenges. One of the challenges is to be a whole person and yet to freely give of the self to the other person. It involves living for oneself, but at the same time, living outside oneself. It means saying, "This is what I want," while asking "What do you want?" In the process of working through these seeming paradoxes, each becomes more of a person. Someday, we hope Bruce can experience all of that.

Our goal for our marriage—and our hope for yours —is the same as the apostle Paul's prayer for the church at Philippi. "That our love may abound more and more in knowledge and depth of insight, so that we may be able to discern what is best."[1]

That discernment means that we must understand each other's personality and each other's past and then build our relationship on the building blocks of caregiving, forgiveness, and mutuality. We are learning to be partners in intimacy. You can too.

Appendix 1

An Explanation of the Dominant Process

MANY WHO HAVE attended our seminars say, "I know it's complicated, but tell me anyway. We want to know how you know which function is dominant." How do you figure it out?" Here's one way.

1. The dominant function comes from one of the two middle letters of the four which represent your preferences. It is either the second letter, *S* or *N* (the perceiving process); or it can be the third letter, *T* or *F* (the judging process).

2. To decide which of these two processes is dominant, it is necessary to look at the fourth letter (either *J*, judging, or *P*, perceiving). If your last letter is *J*, it tells us that the judging process (either *T* or *F*) is dominant in the external world. If your last letter is *P*, it tells us that the perceiving process (either *S* or *N*) is dominant in the external world. For example, if your letters are *ESTJ*, the *J* at the end tells us that the judging process, in this case is the thinking function (*T*), is dominant. Or if your letters are *ESTP*, the *P* at the end tells us that the perceiving process, in this case the sensing function (*S*), is dominant.

3. Now that sounds simple enough, but there is one complication. We are trying to determine which of the functions is dominant—that is, which is the biggest room in our personality house. Step two tells us how to find the dominant process in the external world by looking at the *J* or *P*, but it is important to know that it

tells us what the dominant process is only if we are extraverted (*E* as the first letter). For extraverts, the formula works. The dominant process that we determined from step two is what you show to the world. Remember that expressive extraverts relate to an outer world of people and things, and so they show their dominant process to the world. It is their first step forward, so to speak.

4. But for introverts (those of you who have an *I* as your first letter), it is a different story. Introverts do not tend to show their dominant process to the outside world. Introverted (*I*) people relate primarily to an inner world of thoughts and ideas. So their dominant process is used mostly in that inner world and is hidden from most of the outside world. For them, the dominant process is determined in an opposite way than for the extravert *(E)*.

5. To determine the dominant process for the introvert, look again at the fourth letter, either *J* or *P*. If the introvert (*I*) has a *J*, his or her dominant process in the external world is the judging process, but the true dominant process in his or her internal world is the perceiving process, either the *S* or *N*, whichever is the second letter (the opposite for the extravert). For example, if your letters are *INFJ*, the *J* at the end tells us that your dominant function in the external world is the *F* (feeling), but that the true dominant function, which you use in your internal world is the *N* (the intuitive function—golden eagle). It is dominant, but hidden to the outside world. And if you are an introvert (*I*) and have a *P* at the end, your dominant process is either the *T* or *F*, whichever letter occupies the third space in your four letters. Here the judging function (either *T* or *F*) is dominant (opposite for the extravert), but again hidden to the outside world. For example, if your letters are *INFP*, the *P* at the end tells

us that your dominant function is the *F* (the feeling function—green mouse), the third letter, but it is usually hidden to the outside world.

6. Then what do you call what introverts show to the outside world? They show what is called their auxiliary process. They depend on the auxiliary process to relate to and communicate with the world. The auxiliary process is found in the introvert (*I*) by determining the true dominant process (Step 5), and then finding what other middle letter or function is there. For example, as above, if your letters are *INFJ*, your true dominant function in your internal world is the *N*, and the other middle letter left is *F*. So in this case, the *F* (feeling function) is the auxiliary, which is shown to the outside world. If your letters are *INFP*, the dominant function is the *F*, and the other middle letter is *N*, so in this case the auxiliary is the *N* (intuitive function) and is what the *INFP* shows to the world. His dominant process, the feeling function, is hidden. When you meet him you will see his auxiliary, the intuitive function.

7. For the extravert (*E*) the auxiliary process is used in his inner world. When you meet the extravert, you meet his or her dominant, and he sometimes will show you his auxiliary. The auxiliary for the extravert is determined in the same way it was for the introvert. Find the letter (Step 2) designating the dominant, and then look at the other middle letter; this will tell you the auxiliary. For example, if your letters are *ESTJ*, your dominant function, as we determined above, is the *T*, which leaves the other middle letter, *S* (sensing function), as the auxiliary. If your letters are *ESTP*, your dominant function will be the *S*, and the auxiliary will be the *T* (thinking function).

Notes

Chapter 1. The Intimacy Puzzle

1. Caryl S. Avery, "How do you build intimacy in an age of divorce?" *Psychology Today,* May 1989, 27.
2. "The Great Experiment," special edition, *Time,* Fall 1990, 72ff.
3. Judith Wallerstein and Sandra Blakeslee, *Second Chances: Men, Women and Children a Decade After Divorce* (New York: Ticknor & Fields, 1989), 5.

Chapter 3. Extravert or Introvert Relator?

1. Isabell Briggs-Meyers with Peter Briggs, *Gifts Differing* (Palo Alto, CA: Consulting Psychologists Press, 1980), 54.

Chapter 4. Sensing or Intuitive Observer?

1. Wallerstein and Blakeslee, *Second Chances,* 58.

Chapter 5. Thinking or Feeling Decision Maker?

1. Meyers with Briggs, *Gifts Differing,* 66.
2. (Note 2)

Chapter 6. Judging or Perceiving Organizer?

1. Avril Thorne and Harrison Gough, *Portraits of Types* (Palo Alto, CA: Consulting Psychologists Press, 1991), 13.

Chapter 8. The Destructive Traditions of Our Childhood Families

1. These stories are told in Genesis 12-50.
2. Genesis 27:42.

253

3. Exodus 20:5; Exodus 34:7.
4. Genesis 20.
5. Genesis 26:6-11.

Chapter 9. Our Parents' Impact on Our Ability to Trust and Be Trusted

1. See David Stoop and James Masteller, *Forgiving Our Parents, Forgiving Ourselves* (Ann Arbor, MI: Servant Publications, 1991), 169-79.

Chapter 11. Forgiveness

1. Matthew 6:12, 14-15.
2. Ephesians 4:32.

Chapter 12. The Give-and-Take of Mutuality

1. Paraphrase of Philippians 1:9-11 NIV.